Tax Havens

TAX HAVENS

Anthony Sanfield Ginsberg

NEW YORK INSTITUTE OF FINANCE

NEW YORK • TORONTO • SYDNEY • TOKYO • SINGAPORE

Library of Congress Cataloging-in-Publication Data

Ginsberg, Anthony S.
    Tax havens / Anthony S. Ginsberg.
        p.   cm.
    Includes index.
    ISBN 0-13-886649-X
    1. Tax havens.   2. Tax planning.   3. Tax planning—United
States.
    I. Title.
    K4464.5.G56   1991   91-16367
    336.2'06—dc20   CIP

Printed in the United States of America

10   9   8   7   6

This publication is designed to provide accurate and authoritative information in regard to the subject matter covered. It is sold with the understanding that the publisher is not engaged in rendering legal, accounting, or other professional service. If legal advice or other expert assistance is required, the services of a competent professional person should be sought.
—From the *Declaration of Principles jointly adopted by a Committee of the American Bar Association and a Committee of Publishers and Associations*

ISBN 0-13-886649-X

 NEW YORK INSTITUTE OF FINANCE
2 Broadway
New York, N.Y. 10004-2283
(212) 859-5000
A Simon & Schuster Company

On the World Wide Web at http://www.phdirect.com

Prentice-Hall International (UK) Limited, *London*
Prentice-Hall of Australia Pty. Limited, *Sydney*
Prentice-Hall Canada Inc., *Toronto*
Prentice-Hall Hispanoamericana, S.A., *Mexico*
Prentice-Hall of India Private Limited, *New Delhi*
Prentice-Hall of Japan, Inc., *Tokyo*
Simon & Schuster Asia Pte. Ltd., *Singapore*
Editora Prentice-Hall do Brasil, Ltda., *Rio de Janeiro*

To the most important people
in my life—
Mom and Dad
Dean and Caryn

Contents

Preface

This book is divided into three parts. Part One focuses on the general elements of the tax haven system: their growth and importance, how they can be used, different structures for tax haven usage, their benefits, and their role in international finance.

Part Two is a more specific discussion of ten representative tax havens and their attributes. This Part examines the Cayman Islands, Liechtenstein, Luxembourg, the Channel Islands (Jersey and Guernsey), the Isle of Man, Hong Kong, Gibraltar, Madeira, and the Bahamas. Although some readers may fear that I have neglected a favorite tax haven, they should bear in mind that many tax havens have similar characteristics and that the ten havens examined here are each representative in some way of other popular havens. Part Two also considers the creation of a barrier-free market in the European Community in 1992 and the likely effects of the proposed harmonization of the tax systems of the member states.

Part Three examines considerations of specific interest to U.S. taxpayers and how the U.S. tax system affects the use of tax havens.

I hope that everyone who reads this book takes home some new thoughts and ideas. I would be happy to receive any comments.

Acknowledgment

The idea of assembling all the material I had gathered, into book form, occurred to me after completing a dissertation at the University of Cape Town.

There are many people whom I wish to acknowledge for their help, support, and motivation throughout the time that I was working on this book. Unfortunately, I can mention only a handful of them, and I do this with some trepidation.

I would like to acknowledge my immediate family: Mom, Dad, Dean, Caryn, and my two grandmothers; my close friends Richard, Lance, Debbie, Jerome; Arthur Andersen, and Horwarth & Horwarth; the University of Cape Town; Fairheads Trust, and all those who helped me in any special way to complete this book.

Without the exceptional kindness and understanding of Beverly and Warren Lieberman, this book might have been a figment of my imagination. They, more importantly, than any others, gave me the opportunity to make a new life for myself in the United States. I will never forget all their help.

There have been many special people that I have come to know since arriving in the United States at the end of 1989. The great friendship of my best American buddies—David Birnbaum and Marshall (Mumbles) Starkman, and their families—has been an important key to my survival in New York and to the final completion of this book.

I would like to thank my roommates, Paul and Shawn, for their understanding throughout the months of writing the manuscript. To Graham, it's been very special knowing someone from my part of the world, who has survived six years in New York City—thanks for all your help and support.

I extend sincere thanks for the assistance and understanding shown by my fellow analysts at Salomon Brothers Inc. Special thanks to Michael Gottdenker for his continued support.

Finally, I would like to express my appreciation to all the governments of the jurisdictions covered in this book for their help and cooperation.

PART ONE

The Elements of the Tax Haven System

1

Introduction

The term "tax havens" covers three classes of jurisdiction:

1. Countries where there are no relevant taxes (tax paradises such as the Cayman Islands, the Bahamas, and Bermuda);

2. Countries where taxes are levied only on internal taxable events, but not at all, or at very low rates, on profits from foreign sources (tax shelters such as Hong Kong, and Panama); and

3. Countries where special tax privileges are granted to certain types of companies or operations (such as the Channel Islands, Liechtenstein, Luxembourg, the Isle of Man, and Monaco).

The principal function of tax havens is the avoidance of current and future taxes and exchange controls. However, tax havens may also serve to postpone the imposition of tax, thus permitting the more rapid development and consolidation of an undertaking. Furthermore, tax havens often provide an effective shield against sanctions and against the dangers of confiscation, nationalization, and other types of expropriation.

International tax planning has rightly become a central strategy in modern commercial life, and the sensible exploitation of tax

3

havens lies at its core. However, the rewards expected of an international plan can quickly become liabilities if the plan is poorly conceived.

Consider the example of a U.S. company that trades worldwide. Having heard that Hong Kong levies tax on profits at the rate of 17%, the company decides to establish a Hong Kong company to enable it to avoid the U.S. tax of 34%. From then on, all invoices are made out in the name of the Hong Kong company, but management is exercised from the United States. The U.S. company begins to forecast greatly increased gross income for the organization, but it will soon learn that it has made a fundamental error by not investigating all of the implications of its plan. First, it has failed to consider that there is no double-taxation agreement between the United States and Hong Kong, so that profits taxed in Hong Kong may also be taxed in the United States when they are repatriated. Moreover, by retaining management and control of the Hong Kong company in the United States, it has neglected the provisions of U.S. law that makes the place of management and control a vital factor in determining whether an international enterprise will be subject to U.S. tax. Therefore, this company's misconceived plan may well subject the enterprise to taxation in both Hong Kong and the United States at a combined rate higher than would have been paid if the plan had not been implemented in the first place.

IMPLEMENTING AN INTERNATIONAL TAX PLAN

Choice of a Tax Haven

With respect to the payment of taxes, tax havens fall into two general categories: those that levy no taxes at all, or at least no tax on a particular type of income, and those that levy very low taxes. The latter can be advantageous for three reasons. First, foreign-source income is sometimes exempted in the recipient's country of residence *if and only if* it has borne tax at the source. This applies, for example, to dividends received by a Netherlands holding company from its non-Dutch holdings or to the foreign branch profits of an Australian company. In both cases, income derived from a tax-free area would be subject to tax at home at rates in excess of 40%, while income derived from a country imposing a low rate of tax would be exempt. Clearly, in such cases there is everything to be said for paying some local tax rather than none. Second, there is often an advantage in routing dividends, interest, or royalties into a country that imposes some taxes, but that enjoys the benefit of a double-taxation agreement that reduces the rate of tax at source. This may result in a lower aggregate tax charge than could be achieved by using a zero-tax intermediary.

A third important feature of jurisdictions that impose low taxes as against zero tax, is that these jurisdictions are reviewed in a more favorable light and are often the base for foreign operations of well-established multinationals. Western democratic governments often show much more restraint and less interest in investigating the affairs of companies incorporated in such jurisdictions.

Off-shore financial centers are commonly perceived to be tax havens, and in many instances this is correct. Although some territories qualify as both off-shore centers and as tax havens, it is perhaps easier to categorize off-shore centers as countries that offer special advantages to companies and provide an international corporation with greater freedom of action than might be possible if it were tied to a single national base. Tax havens, however, offer special tax advantages to private persons and companies.

It is impossible to provide a concise or exhaustive definition of what exactly constitutes an international off-shore financial center. While many countries, especially those properly regarded as tax havens, provide international organizations with such a range of tax-planning opportunities that all professional tax advisers would regard them as international off-shore centers, other jurisdictions have far fewer features capable of exploitation in international tax planning, and advisers may disagree as to whether they ought to be regarded as off-shore centers. Many off-shore centers may fairly be described as tax havens due to their extraordinarily low income tax rates. Such tax havens are typically very small countries that in some cases have deliberately created a virtually tax-free environment to encourage the use of the jurisdiction as a conduit in international transactions.

However, many other off-shore financial centers are major commercial jurisdictions with high rates of tax and sophisticated taxation systems. The latter usually qualify as off-shore financial centers due to peculiarities of their legal and taxations systems that permit them to be used effectively in international tax planning despite their high internal tax rates. Switzerland is probably the best-known example of a highly sophisticated regime that through a confluence of factors has become an international financial center, even though its federal, cantonal, and municipal rates often exceed 40% in the aggregate.

Lord Palmerston, the nineteenth century British Foreign Secretary, once lamented that Queen Victoria's colonies were multiplying so fast he had to "keep looking the damned places up on the map." Today's international investors, bankers, and fund managers could be forgiven for echoing that sentiment as they survey the world's off-shore financial centers. From Andorra to Vanuatu, from Monaco to Montevideo, an increasing number of islands, ministates, and developing countries are promoting themselves as tax havens, hoping to cash in on a growing industry. Nowhere is the competition more intense or the field more crowded than the Caribbean, which has garnered a substantial slice of this global multibillion-dollar business.

It should be remembered that most of this business exists on paper only. Transactions and decisions are usually made in the great cities of the world and instructions are relayed off-shore, where lawyers, accountants, bankers, and bureaucrats take care of the paperwork and occasionally act as hosts to visiting clients. Apart from tourism, most of these off-shore territories are not economically advanced. Lacking natural resources, capital, and manpower, they generally have no significant agricultural or industrial base and are dependent on the outside world for supplies.

Off-shore business generates foreign exchange, tax revenues, and employment, as well as indirect benefits. It offers a chance of economic diversification and is far more profitable than tourism once the necessary infrastructure is in place, requiring less manpower and foreign exchange spending. Moreover, even a moderate degree of success can have a big impact in the smaller economies.

Since World War II, the demand for off-shore financial services has grown rapidly as a result of a combination of high taxation and proliferating regulations in the industrialized countries and political instability elsewhere. The rise of multinational companies, whose primary allegiance is to shareholders, not nations, has counseled them to use tax haven jurisdictions as a catalyst for world trade. By recent estimates, 50% of all money processed internationally goes through tax havens. Were it not for the existence of tax havens, the cost of most goods owned and produced by multinational groups would be higher and there would be greater unemployment. It should be remembered that it is "against the religion" of multinationals to pay tax. Thus, their weight in the world of tax havens is the most important consideration for governments attempting to attract them to their shores. This investment in tax havens has been made possible by revolutionary advances in technology and communications, which have erased the barriers of time and space for even the most remote locations.

Until recently, off-shore financial centers were commonly described as tax havens, a term that many off-shore players dislike because it suggests that they help people to circumvent the laws of other countries. But the term accurately reflects the origins of the business and remains a condition of its continued existence. No off-shore center could hope to survive if it imposed normal levels of taxation.

Tax Evasion or Tax Planning

Tax evasion is probably one of man's oldest pastimes, and there is little doubt that off-shore centers are used for this purpose. But most off-shore activities could be described as tax planning, using legal mechanisms to reduce or eliminate taxes on income, wealth, profits, and inheritance or to accumulate tax-free income off-shore pending registration of a taxable jurisdiction.

Such arrangements are often used when the income or assets in question are of an international nature. For example, an author who receives royalties from many countries may have them paid to a tax haven until he needs them. Cross-border mutual funds may be registered off-shore to minimize taxation and boost returns. In many cases, ultimately some tax is paid in the home country of the business or individual, but off-shore tax haven strategies can help maximize after-tax returns, permitting repatriation at the most beneficial time.

More complex considerations arise for residents of countries such as the United States which levy tax on a worldwide basis irrespective of whether income is repatriated. But here, too, there are legal possibilities available off-shore. For example, although U.S. banks must pay U.S. taxes on the profits of their branches worldwide, they may claim credit for taxes paid to other countries, reducing their U.S. tax liability. However, the amount of credit allowed is limited. To avoid accumulating excess credit in high-tax countries and to lower their foreign tax rate in general, these banks book some of their loans in tax-free off-shore centers. As a bonus, the income on such loans is often exempt from state and local taxes in the United States because the business is entirely international.

It should be noted that tax efficiency is not the only reason for using a tax haven. Freedom from regulation is a major attraction, and it is no coincidence that banking, insurance, and ship registration are three of the pillars of tax haven business. Furthermore, tax havens can allow diversification into many activities not permitted at home or assist in creating a level playing field in circumstances where a company is subject to heavy regulation in its own country while its foreign competitors are not. A prime example of the avoidance of regulation is the use of tax havens by American and Japanese banks to engage in the securities business, which is denied them at home.

Often the lack of compatibility between the tax regimes of different countries can give rise to anomalous situations that make a foreign business operation too expensive to develop. An extreme example of this incompatibility is the double taxation of profits. This may occur where profits of a foreign subsidiary business are fully taxed in the foreign country; then those same after-tax profits, when repatriated to the home country by way of dividend, are subject to be taxed again as income of the parent. Unless a credit of some kind is available for the taxes already paid by the foreign subsidiary, double

taxation would inevitably render the activities of
expensive to pursue. In one instance, the withdr
agreement between South Africa and the United Su.
the disinvestment of many U.S. foreign subsidiaries. A smu_r
structuring of the subsidiaries' headquarters to Windhoek (Namibia)
would be sufficient to avoid any double taxation. As of Namibia's
independence, all U.S. corporations are given credit for taxes incurred there. Any branches in South Africa would most probably take
advantage of a Namibia-South Africa tax treaty. An effective international tax strategy must take into account not only the interaction
of the tax regimes applicable to the parent company and its off-shore
subsidiary, but also the possibilities of utilizing companies in third
countries, which may allow the overall tax incurred by the corporate
grouping to be reduced.

Some anomalies arise because some countries assess tax on a
source basis only, such as Hong Kong, while most Western countries
assess tax on a residence or citizenship basis or a combination of all
three. By utilizing a tax haven entity, significant tax savings can be
achieved as a consequence of these differing criteria for imposing tax
liabilities. For example, profits earned by an entity could be shifted
from country A to the tax haven without incurring tax simply because
the entity is a nonresident of country A; the same result could be
achieved by ensuring that all profits are sourced in the tax haven
country.

MOTIVATION TO USE A TAX HAVEN

The motives for using a tax haven will vary with each individual case,
but the most common motivating factors and circumstances are the
following:

- High taxes in the country of residence, particularly where a
  progressive system of taxation applies, since progressive taxation has the most impact on individuals in the higher income
  brackets and on those such as entertainment earners who
  have fluctuating income;

- Unfavorable inheritance provisions in the country of residence;
- Employment under contract overseas, particularly in situations where overseas income is free of tax unless remitted to the country of domicile;
- Anonymity and secrecy, particularly through the use of confidential bank accounts, nominees, and bearer shares;
- Political considerations that inhibit individuals or businesses from holding wealth in their country of residence;
- Re-routing of export sales, as in the case of an author or investor, or of overseas purchasing, as in the case of an individual entrepreneur;
- Depositing surplus funds, as in a family trust;
- Accumulating income for retirement or before emigration;
- Geographical expansion of multinational corporations; and
- Protecting an estate from division on divorce.

It should be noted that secrecy may be desirable for reasons other than tax avoidance. Many organizations use tax havens to develop new products or business ideas out of sight of their commercial competitors.

WHY DEVELOPED COUNTRIES TOLERATE TAX HAVENS

The U.S. economy in its desperate search for capital to promote its economy has itself become somewhat of a tax haven for foreigners who invest their money in U.S. banks. No U.S. tax is levied on interest earned in bank deposits made by foreigners. This influx of foreign capital is then used by the U.S. banking system to stimulate the U.S. economy through funding U.S. corporations, homeowners, real estate development, and research and technology.

Many foreign investors to the U.S. economy are able to purchase U.S. corporations, real estate, and bonds at realistic prices as a result of using low-tax bases around the world.

U.S. companies in turn are able to access foreign capital through such markets as Eurobonds and offshore-equity markets.

Through the establishment of offshore-subsidiary finance companies, U.S. companies have established financing bases around the world utilizing substantial international tax benefits such as joint residency (able to claim deductions and losses in two jurisdictions). The U.S. government's willingness to stimulate the economy has been key in maintaining the offshore window for U.S. companies to obtain cheap finance in numerous low-tax jurisdictions worldwide. Foreign incentive programs, such as the Foreign Sales Corporation for U.S. exporters, as well as various other tax deferral benefits are offered so as to strengthen the U.S. balance of payments.

As much as the developed countries may want to prohibit their taxpayers from using tax havens, they cannot without damaging their own national economies or destroying their capital markets.

In the case of national capital markets, the United States does not impose income tax on the interest paid to foreign depositors of U.S. banks. This encourages foreign depositors to leave their money in the United States. If this exemption was eliminated, billions of dollars would leave the banks, and the sudden loss of these funds might effectively destroy New York as a major capital market.

2

Criteria for Choosing a Tax Haven

The common advantages of a tax haven include:

- Freedom from liability for tax;
- Strict laws of secrecy for banking and commercial transactions; and
- No exchange control.

One of the common disadvantages is that typical tax havens seldom enter into tax treaties with other countries. Unfortunately, without the benefit of tax treaties many jurisdictions are unpopular for certain types of companies and individuals to operate out of. The most disadvantageous reason to use such jurisdictions is that any flow of funds (from another jurisdiction that levies tax—most Western nations) received are most often received net of high-withholding taxes imposed by the original/source jurisdictions. Without the benefit of tax treaties the reception of funds (interest, salaries, or dividends) will always be subject to a large withholding tax liability.

Another disadvantage is that the "aura of concealment" that surrounds tax havens may cause domestic tax authorities to monitor their taxpayers more closely. This has certainly been the trend with tax havens in the Caribbean Basin, which have fairly recently concluded agreements with the United States to cooperate in tracing and eradicating tax evasion by U.S. taxpayers.

Tax havens are located throughout the world. The better known of them may be grouped loosely into the following areas:

- The Caribbean area—the Bahamas, Bermuda, the Cayman Islands, the British Virgin Islands, the Netherlands Antilles, and Panama;
- The Mediterranean area—Gibraltar and Cyprus;
- The European area—the Netherlands, Switzerland, Liechtenstein, Andorra, Luxembourg, Campione, and Monaco;
- The Channel Islands area—Guernsey, Jersey, and the Isle of Man;
- The Pacific area—Hong Kong, Vanuatu, and Nauru.

PRINCIPLES OF SELECTION

Professional tax specialists unanimously agree that tax havens are not for everyone. The decision to take advantage of their benefits must be weighed carefully, since there is no so-called standard index to follow.

Of course, the first step in the selection of a tax haven is to analyze the nature and extent of the tax relief offered by various jurisdictions.

Not all tax havens are "pure," in that very few levy no taxes at all. Most offer relief from tax based on the type of income earned, the source of the income, the class of entity or business activity involved, or a combination of these factors. Thus, for example, a country that levies taxes on domestic income alone will be a haven with respect to income derived from foreign sources, and a country that limits its tax base to residents will be a haven with respect to income accruing to nonresidents.

In general terms, relief from taxation can be classified in the following forms:

■ Tax exemption ("no tax" havens): Anguilla, the Bahamas, Bahrain, Bermuda, the Cayman Islands, Cook Islands, Djibouti, Turks and Caicos, Vanuatu.

■ Low taxation (this may be accomplished by fixed rates established by the specific government or in combination with reduced or exempted taxes resulting from treaties to avoid double taxation): Liechtenstein, Oman, Switzerland, Jersey, Guernsey, British Virgin Islands.

■ Tax exemption of foreign-source income (territoriality basis of taxation instead of worldwide source): Hong Kong, Liberia, Panama, Philippines, Venezuela, Shannon International Airport.

■ Special incentive privileges to off-shore companies and qualified holding companies: Luxembourg, the Netherlands, the Netherlands Antilles, Singapore.

■ Tax exemption for manufacturing and processing of exports: Ireland.

■ International business company tax reduction (investment companies considered as privileged off-shore financial companies): Antigua, Barbados, Grenada, Jamaica.

Tax havens vary significantly in terms of the tax-planning opportunities they offer. In addition to tax relief, numerous relevant factors must be considered carefully. The following are the most important fundamental factors that might be considered:

■ Geographic location. Although tax haven operations could be located virtually anywhere in the world, a convenient location may be a factor of importance. For example, a multinational corporation based in France might conclude that one of the European centers is the best location for an off-shore subsidiary because its managers could travel more efficiently between headquarters and the field. Similarly, an individual U.S. investor might find a Caribbean center more convenient. The convenience of using a tax haven close to the center of an individual's or corporation's operations is of specific importance as regards the administration and constant up-to-the minute documentation and reporting requirements.

- Political and economic stability. With the recent unrest in Panama and Liberia focus has been placed more than ever before on a jurisdiction's long-term stability, before setting up any kind of off-shore venture. Only recently has Gibraltar re-appeared as a popular off-shore center, while Hong Kong has suffered from uncertainty as regards 1997. At present, the Cayman Islands can rightfully boast to be the most stable tax haven; as well as benefiting from its relationship as a crown colony of the United Kingdom. Switzerland's neutrality throughout the entire modern era has ensured its demand as a financial gatekeeper.

- Guarantees against future taxes. The Cayman Islands offers attractive guarantees to both exempted trusts and exempted companies—both are exempt from 20 to 50 years from the date of incorporation.

- Conducting of active business in the tax haven itself. This feature enables a subsidiary company to obtain cheap finance from within the tax haven or even make investments in the jurisdictions, such as entering into a syndicate or joint venture in a real estate development.

- Existence of anti-tax avoidance legislation by the parent country. Any planning utilizing tax havens in an international set-up must take cognizance of the tax legislation within the country where the parent/holding company is incorporated. Often, specific tax havens are the targets of a Western government's investigations or tax code thus nullifying any benefit that might arise from utilizing its tax free or low tax base laws.

- Laws governing companies, trusts, and other entities.

- [ ] the speed and ease of establishing, running, and winding up a trust, base company;

- [ ] restrictions on the nationality of shareholders, directors, and other officers, and the ease with which any such restrictions may be overcome by the use of nominees;

- [ ] the place of shareholders' and directors' meetings; and

- [ ] the allowance of bearer shares and of shares without a par value.

- **Secrecy of information.** The Cayman Islands and Liechtenstein make it a criminal offence for tax officials and bank employees to reveal any information coming before them. The fact that the goods might originate in country A or that the ultimate ownership of an overseas company rests in country A can often close doors and jeopardize international operations. The existence of companies in tax havens that act as conduits for the sale of goods originating in country A even though no other commercial reason can be put forward for the existence of such companies—and the issue of bearer shares by companies within the off-shore structure, provided possession of such shares is retained in country A.

- **Flexibility.** Certain tax havens provide that the seat or domicile of a company may be moved out of the jurisdiction in the event of a change of circumstances. The Cayman Islands has such legislation in place. This feature is of vital importance and relates to a jurisdiction's political and economic stability.

- Existence of a tax treaty network or double taxation agreements. Certain havens owe their existence to these networks, while the lack of agreements is beneficial in precluding the furnishing of information to other governments. (See earlier comments about benefit of tax treaties.)

- The tax treatment of nonresident and foreign income.

- What taxes are levied to finance the state.

- The adequacy of banking, professional, commercial, transportation, and communication facilities. The infrastructure of the jurisdiction is vital to the constant upkeep and proper maintenance of the entity. Without adequate professionals to administer the entity, all other benefits offered by the government may be rendered useless.

- Any exchange controls and restrictions. While there are significant advantages in operating in a tax haven that does not have exchange controls, a foreign company can avoid most of the restrictions of exchange controls by maintaining a nonresident status (i.e., by not trading within the jurisdiction).

- Existence of antitax avoidance legislation/government attitude to tax haven operations.

- Requirements for a local office or employees or lack thereof—a new ruling in Luxembourg states that for required funds no physical presence is necessary.

Double-Taxation Treaties

Avoidance of double taxation by both the host government and that of the home country of the foreign investor has been an objective of most nations since negotiation of the first Income Tax Convention in the mid nineteenth century. Today, for example, the United States has 47 of these treaties to avoid double taxation. However, few tax haven countries have been in a position to negotiate tax treaties because an absence of taxes or "colonial territory" status prevent it. The Netherlands has the broadest system of income tax treaties, with agreements concluded with most industrial nations and many developing countries. In fact, international companies frequently choose to establish holding companies in the Netherlands so that their second-tier subsidiaries or branches may take advantage of numerous Dutch tax treaties to avoid or reduce taxation. As such, the Netherlands Antilles has been the most popular choice for establishing a subsidiary company.

Avoidance of Currency Restrictions

In appraising a country's tax haven climate there is hardly a better clue to the host government's attitude and the investor's earnings prospects than the extent of currency and exchange controls. Most businesspeople tend to avoid establishing foreign base operations where currency controls are maintained or are especially complicated. Where currency and exchange restrictions exist, arrangements often may be made with local government authorities to receive exchange for imports of certain raw materials or essential equipment, to pay expenses in local currencies, or to enjoy free transfer of capital, earnings, royalties, and fees.

Import Freedom for Necessary Raw Materials

Since most of the world's developing countries are forced to restrict imports because of exchange shortages, they are at a disadvantage in attracting foreign-base company operations. The foreign tax havens that depend on trading as one of their principal incentives to lure overseas companies cannot afford to inhibit imports. This is particularly true in Panama, Puerto Rico, Ireland, Switzerland, and Vanuatu. Needless to say, if foreign companies cannot import required materials or the equipment to process them, their management will look for other locations. To circumvent this bottleneck, some tax haven countries have adopted special incentive laws exempting imports from controls or quotas. This is normally accomplished by establishing a free trade zone where packaging, labeling, processing, and manufacturing for re-export may be done without subjecting the imported materials to controls on imports or custom duties (e.g., Madeira).

Access to Local Capital

In recent years Luxembourg has sky-rocketed to near the top of the list of preferable sites for foreign-base corporations requiring Eurocurrency funds for their world operations. Encouraged by liberal banking and exchange laws, hundreds of the world's major commercial banks have rushed to establish branch or subsidiary operations in Luxembourg, as well as in the Cayman Islands and Hong Kong.

Some scenarios include:

1. *Exporter to Europe.* A U.S. company wishing to export its product throughout Europe decides to manufacture the last 20% of the product in Maderia. As a result of its relationship with Portugal (which is a member of the European Economic Community), the U.S. company situated in Maderia is able to manufacture its goods free of many European taxes and import duties which it would ordinarily have paid if the production process took place solely in the United States. Madeira has thus acted effectively as a conduit jurisdiction.

2. *Movement of jurisdiction.* An international shipping company registered in Panama is wary of the political upheaval that is to come. As a result of the unforeseen political climate the company is deregistered and registered in Cyprus instead. This was possible as a result of prior planning and the insertion of clauses specifying conditions by which an automatic change of residence was possible.

3 *Tax treaty network.* As a result of the U.S. government's repeal of the majority of the tax treaty between the United States and the Netherlands Antilles, direct use of the Antilles has been curtailed for U.S. multinationals. However, by interposing an international holding company in the Netherlands, a Netherlands Antilles foreign subsidiary can be established to raise cheap funds for the international holding company's operations in Europe; and all interest income received by the Netherlands Antilles company can be remitted back to the Netherlands at minimal withholding tax rate as a result of its tax treaty with the Netherlands. A similar case exists in the use of a British intermediary company owned by a U.S. corporation specifically to take advantage of the British tax treaty with Hong Kong.

Figure 2.1. Smokescreen structure.

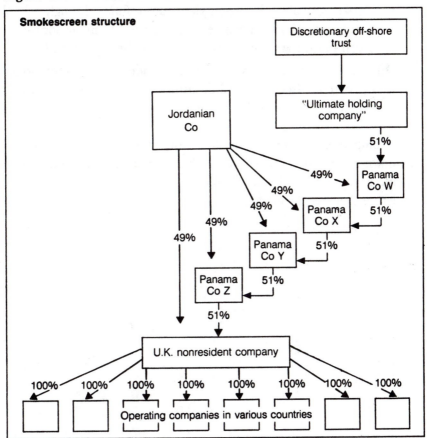

tion, while one based in an obvious tax haven, such as the Cayman Islands, may do so.

■ Swiss numbered accounts offer little security for a truly anonymous account since Swiss secrecy laws have been weakened by international pressure against tax evasion and crime.

■ Trusts remain an enormously powerful instrument. For example, because damages in liability suits have spiraled to astronomical amounts, some surgeons in the United States now divert their wealth into trusts in off-shore havens beyond the reach of U.S. courts.

■ Sometimes a very unusual jurisdiction can be used to make a trial "go cold." For example, routing funds through a bank account in Finland can be used to stymie U.S. authorities, as can one in Argentina in the case of the British authorities.

■ Free ports can be very useful to hide a country of origin. There are free ports in Mauritius, Madeira, Taiwan, Ireland, Hong Kong, and the Bahamas.

Companies that import products into the United States but are incorporated in countries viewed with suspicion, such as Jordan, Lebanon, Nicaragua, and Iraq, would be prime users of the following structure depicted in Figure 2.1.

3

Financial Techniques for Using Tax Havens

Any company engaged in overseas operations is fully entitled to expect tax savings if it plans carefully. However, to ensure that the overseas structure is not subject to attack by tax authorities throughout the world, it is essential that the plan have substance. To achieve substance, the plan may require, for example, the establishment of a holding company with permanent offices and employees overseas, which may require substantial capital investment. Moreover, if all contingencies are not considered, apparent tax savings may prove illusory. Thus, before any international tax plan is implemented, a thorough cost-benefit analysis should be made.

Generally, four fundamental techniques are used in formulating an international tax plan incorporating tax havens:

- Distributing post-tax profits through jurisdictions with double-taxation agreements;
- Allocating pre-tax profits to a low-tax jurisdiction;
- Profit extraction; and
- Minimizing taxes on executive remuneration.

Other techniques are available for more specific situations.

DISTRIBUTION OF POST-TAX PROFITS

The most relevant and permanent savings can usually be achieved by minimizing withholding taxes deducted from dividend distributions paid to foreign shareholders. The technique generally involves interposing holding companies located in countries with numerous favorable double-taxation agreements (DTAs) or with unilateral tax relief relating to dividend income.

A country that has numerous favorable DTAs is obviously a good choice for the home of the interposed company, especially if the foreign operation spans more than one jurisdiction. One example of such a country is the Netherlands, which has entered into no fewer than 30 DTAs. The following example illustrates the advantages and pitfalls in tax planning for international operations.

A Hungarian holding company wishes to establish a subsidiary in the United States. Savings of withholding tax can be achieved by interposing a Netherlands holding company between the Hungarian holding company and its U.S. subsidiary. If a Netherlands company is not interposed, the U.S. withholding tax levied on dividends would be 30%. However, by interposing a Netherlands company, withholding tax of only 5% would be levied on dividends declared by the U.S. company to the Dutch company. In turn, the Dutch company would have to deduct a further withholding tax of 4.75% (5% of 95%) on dividends paid to its Hungarian parent, giving a total withholding of 9.75% and a saving of some 20.25% of the dividend. This saving can be further increased by interposing a company resident in the Netherlands Antilles between the Netherlands and Hungarian companies.

First, the DTA between the Netherlands and the Netherlands Antilles provides for a small withholding tax on dividends between the two countries. The Netherlands Antilles, in turn, has its own favorable unilateral tax legislation, which does not provide for withholding taxes on dividends payments but does levy a corporate tax of 3% on dividends received. This would increase the saving to 22.25%.

SOURCE ALLOCATION OF PRE-TAX PROFITS

Exploiting price differentials is a very useful tax-saving technique, but it is not a device for the greedy. A common example of this technique is an exporting company located in a high-tax jurisdiction that sells its products at a relatively low profit margin to a subsidiary operating in a tax haven. The subsidiary then resells the products at a higher price, thereby trapping profits free of tax in the tax haven.

This technique can often be employed usefully in an international group structure that provides for the movement of products from one country to another. In this type of structure, the source allocation of pre-tax profits is normally achieved by interposing "selling companies," located in tax havens, through which the products are routed. The selling prices of the products are set carefully and allow for a price differential to accrue to the company located in the tax haven. These profits would otherwise have been subject to tax in the country that imported or exported the products. However, because the profits are earned in the tax haven, the tax that would have been imposed is avoided.

Tax authorities worldwide are acutely aware of this technique and have strengthened the anti-avoidance provisions in their tax legislation to counter this potential loss of tax revenue. However, the tax benefit arising from the source allocation of profits to a tax haven can still be obtained if the following four factors are taken into account:

1. *Substance.* It is important to ensure that the existence and location of the selling company can be justified commercially and that it performs a real function within the group as a result of which profits are earned;

2. *Permanent establishment.* This requirement is found in most DTAs; a permanent establishment will subject the profits attributable to that enterprise to tax in the country in which it is located;

3. *Transfer pricing.* It is essential to be able to justify on a commercial basis the various selling prices charged that result in the source allocation of income to a tax haven; if sales

volumes are large, the tax savings attributable to the small price differential can be substantial; and

4. *Management and control.* The site of actual management and control of the selling company must be or appear to be in the tax haven.

Thus, for a company in a high-tax jurisdiction to successfully employ the source-allocation technique, it is clear that it must address several considerations before it includes a selling company in its international group structure. At a minimum, the company must take the following steps:

■ Give substance to the selling company to assure that there are sound commercial reasons for its existence.

■ Find a location convenient to the selling area, since an appropriate location is likely to provide geographic justification for the existence of the company.

■ Examine carefully relevant legislation in the country chosen to ensure that the consequences of incorporation in that country will benefit the international group.

■ Weigh the advantages of using a selling company against the cost of setting up and administering the company.

■ Consider the effects of a permanent establishment, management, and transfer pricing in great detail.

Establishing Management and Control

The place of incorporation is not the decisive test for the tax residence of a company. Even though a company is registered in the Bahamas, if all it does there is maintain a brass plate and a group of dummy directors, it is inviting scrutiny. If the real owners or managers live in a high-tax country, the revenue authorities of that country will try to establish that the company is really resident there. Under British and U.S. tax law, for example, residence for tax purposes is located "where the real business is carried on, where the central management and control actually abides." If this is held to be in the United States or the United Kingdom, the company will be liable to tax in exactly the same way as a locally incorporated company, despite a registered address in the tax haven. In order to avoid this, the Board of Directors must meet and management decisions must appear to be made in the tax haven, or at least outside the high-tax country.

Manufacturing in a Tax Haven

Tax havens can be used as actual manufacturing centers. For this, it may be more advantageous to combine freedom from tax with a free port or customs-free area. The fantastic booms in Hong Kong and Freeport, Bahamas, are a tribute to the enormous release of energy that takes place even in an otherwise inconvenient area when profits can be made and enjoyed without worrying about the tax consequences. Tax holidays, capital allowances, and soft loan facilities in countries that otherwise have high taxes, such as the Republic of Ireland, can also be attractive. The technique of tax-haven manufacture is often most effective when it is applied to a key component or final assembly. If local conditions are favorable to a certain manufacturing operation, a plant may be established in a tax haven to manufacture and sell or lease its products to the parent company without tax liability. Also, such a tax-haven company can organize to manage the foreign sales of the parent company, thus minimizing taxes in the parent company's country of residence. As always, the object of the exercise must be to maximize after-tax profits, which is not necessarily the same as minimizing tax.

PROFIT EXTRACTION

Profits earned in a high-tax country can sometimes be extracted to tax havens as interest, royalties, or management charges. In all these cases, the high-tax country of source is likely to have rules limiting the effectiveness of the technique. The object here is to arrange for payments to be made that are an allowable deduction against taxable profits in the country of origin, thus reducing the taxable profits there. There may be withholding taxes in the country of origin and taxes in the country of receipt, but as long as these total less than the tax that would have been levied on the profits against which the payments are charged, there will be a net advantage.

Double-taxation agreements (DTAs) affect the ways in which dividends, interest, and royalties extracted from third countries are taxed. For example, if a British company pays dividends to American or Swiss shareholders, withholding tax is limited to 15%. If dividends are paid to a shareholder resident in a country that imposes no tax and is not a party to any double-taxation agreement, withholding tax will be at the full standard rate. The full standard rate reflects the withholding tax rate when no DTA exists. This withholding rate can be as much as 30%. As tax havens are most often not party to DTA's with major developed countries—the standard withholding tax rate of 30% is most often suffered if no intermediary company is set up between a major developed country, such as the United States or United Kingdom, and the tax haven. If a U.S. company pays dividends to a U.K. shareholder, withholding tax is limited to 15% and there is no withholding tax on interest and royalties. Payments to a tax haven country suffer 30% in the above cases. Thus, an important group of tax haven operations rests on the proper exploitation of double-taxation agreements, and more sophisticated operations involve countries that levy some tax but which are parties to double-taxation agreements.

A second profit-extraction device employs cross-licensing via Switzerland. In this case, royalties can flow from the United States to Switzerland free of withholding tax under the double-taxation agreement, but profits derived from there will be subject to tax in Switzerland. Switzerland, however, imposes no withholding tax on royalties flowing out. Therefore, patents or copyrights could be transferred to a Liechtenstein company, which would then license a Swiss intermediate company, which in turn would sub-license and receive royalties from the United States. No withholding tax would be paid on either of the royalty flows. Although the Swiss company would be liable to Swiss taxes on profits, royalties paid out would be allowable as a deduction, and little or nothing would remain to be taxed.

Figure 3.1. Direct flow of royalties to the United States.

Royalty remitted from Eastern Europe	$150,000
Less: Withholding tax in Eastern Europe	45,000
Amount remitted to the United States	105,000
Less: U.S. corporate tax on $150,000	51,000
Net amount received in the United States	$ 54,000

Figures 3.1 and 3.2 illustrate the potential benefit that can be achieved by using double-taxation agreements to reduce the impact of withholding taxes. In Figure 3.1, a U.S. company has developed a technological process that it licenses to a subsidiary incorporated in Eastern Europe. All royalties are paid directly to the United States. Even though withholding taxes are paid in Eastern Europe, the IRS will not allow a credit for foreign taxes paid.

In Figure 3.2, the U.S. company acts to reduce the impact of the lost credit for foreign taxes by taking advantage of the numerous double-taxation agreements entered into by the Netherlands. It sells its technological process to a Netherlands subsidiary, which grants a license to the subsidiary in Eastern Europe. The flow of payments would then be as follows:

■ Subroyalty payments would be made from Eastern Europe free of any withholding tax.

■ The Netherlands tax authorities would impute that a "profit" of approximately 7% of the gross royalties were made in the Netherlands. Even if that amount was not retained in the Netherlands, tax at a rate of 48% would be levied on the imputed profit. It is recommended, therefore, that the various licensing agreements provide that 7% of the total royalty charged by the Netherlands company be retained as subroyalty payments in the Netherlands company and 93% be passed to the United States company as its royalty payments.

Figure 3.2. Flow of royalties through subsidiaries.

	Royalty remitted from Eastern Europe	$150,000
Less:	Withholding tax in Eastern Europe	—
	Amount received in the Netherlands	150,000
Less:	Netherlands retention (7%)	10,500
	Royalty remitted to the United States	139,500
	Dividend from Netherlands (Net after tax)	5,460
	Amount remitted to the United States	144,960
Less:	U.S. corporate tax on $150,000	51,000
Add:	Foreign Tax Credit	3,570
Less:	Annual cost of maintaining subsidiaries	1,000
	Net amount received in the United States	$ 96,530

The remaining portion can then be remitted to the United States as a dividend with a small withholding tax.

- The 7% imputed profit in the Netherlands could then be passed onto the Netherlands Antilles, suffering only a 3% tax charge.
- A corporation tax charge of up to 3% would be levied on the royalty and dividend received in the Netherlands Antilles.
- Profits would then be remitted to the United States in the form of dividends, which are not subject to withholding tax.

A total saving of $42,530 has occurred. The net amount prior to any planning that was remitted to the United States was $54,000 and after interposing a Netherlands company so as to take advantage of its tax treaty network, $96,530 were remitted to the United States.

A third profit-extraction device employs paying for management services provided by affiliates abroad or making salary and compensation payments to officers who have provided management services to a foreign entity.

The arrangement depicted in Figure 3.3 illustrates this technique. When the Parent Company A sends executives to work outside the home country, they are employed by the Management Services Com-

Figure 3.3. Extraction of management services payments.

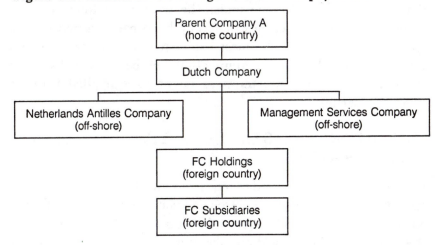

pany, an off-shore subsidiary of the Dutch Holding Company. Over the years, the Home Country group has developed various work manuals and methods for both manufacturing and marketing operations, and these are made available to the Foreign Country (FC) group.

The Management Services Company will supply the services of the Home Country group's executives when they work in a foreign country at a fee that will give the Management Services Company a margin of profit between the fee it receives and the salary it pays. The Home Country group will assign to the Netherlands Antilles company the territorial rights to the know-how contained in its work manuals. These rights will be sublicensed to the Dutch company, which will unlicense them to the various companies in the Foreign Country group that utilize the know-how contained in the manuals. In this way, the FC group will be making tax deductible management fee and royalty payments, which will be taxed at a relatively low rate on ultimate receipt by the Management Services and Netherlands Antilles subsidiaries, respectively.

When using any profit-extraction device, it is vital to maintain the appearance of "arm's length" transactions, especially when undertaking arrangements between related parties, such as companies in an international group. The transactions between these companies will come under the scrutiny of interested tax authorities, who will ensure that they have been carried out on an arm's length basis. The most common test of an arm's length transaction is whether the transaction has been carried out on the same conditions and terms as might have applied between unrelated parties.

MINIMIZING TAXES ON EXECUTIVE REMUNERATION

Executives are often required to render worldwide services to an international group of companies. Double-taxation agreements (DTAs) and other advantageous foreign tax laws can be exploited to minimize the taxes that must be paid on salaries and compensation earned by such executives. This technique focuses on the place of the executive's residence and the amount of time spent by that executive within specific countries.

Tax savings can be achieved by structuring the remuneration package of the executive to shift income to a low-tax jurisdiction. However, it is vital that the remuneration package reflects the substance of the services performed and does not merely maximize tax advantages without taking into account the realities of the situation.

It is common for countries to impose a withholding tax on dividend distributions made by a resident company to its foreign holding company. There is a network of DTAs between various countries that alleviates the problem of high withholding taxes. If a country with suitable DTAs can be interposed between the foreign operating company and the United States holding company, these taxes can frequently be reduced.

TRUSTS

The essence of a trust is that it breaks the chain of legal ownership between the creator of the settlement and his wealth. U.S. tax rules are particularly tough in this regard. Nevertheless, even the IRS can be avoided through the concept of a grantor trust, where the deemed owner of a trust's assets in terms of U.S. law is a person who is neither a U.S. citizen nor a resident of that country. In this case distributions to a beneficiary who is an American citizen or resident are considered as gifts and therefore not taxable in the beneficiary's hands.

Nondiscretionary trusts bind the trustee to the precise instructions of the settlor and confer legally enforceable entitlements on the beneficiaries. With discretionary trusts, however, which are more widely used in international tax planning, the individual beneficiaries do not have vested interests. Instead, the trustee is given wide discretion over the investment of trust funds and distributions to beneficiaries. Normally the settlor will advise the trustee regarding the preferred investments required and the trustee is legally bound not to squander or misappropriate such assets or income. The benefit of this type of trust (discretionary) is that due to the absence of vested interests, a beneficiary will not be considered to own a taxable interest in the underlying funds until such time as he receives a distribution.

Trusts are particularly flexible structures and are often used in a variety of ways. Examples extend from an immigrant into the United States who establishes a trust in a tax haven prior to his residence in the United States, to Orient-Express Company Ltd. which owns a trust (or *stifung*) in Liechtenstein to control some of its hotels in Europe. Often by setting up a trust the beneficiary is able to transfer his wealth, in secret and facilitate global expansion with limited tax costs. This effective method of hiding the ownership of an underlying company by interposing a discretionary type trust between the beneficiaries and the underlying companies they own is most often found where a trust has set up jurisdictions, such as the Isle of Man or the Cayman Islands, that permit bearer shares companies, where ownership is thus anonymous and untraceable. In addition to permitting bearer share companies these jurisdictions often offer incentives to trust owners such as exempt-tax status in the case of the Cayman Islands for up to 50 years, guaranteed.

It is important to remember that the Anglo-Saxon trust is merely a bundle of rights and obligations in equity and thus, strictly speaking, not a legal entity. Although the law of trusts varies from system to system, trusts patterned on the English law of trusts resemble one another closely, and any differences are usually statutory. In the case of civil law systems, such few trust forms that exist are authorized by statute.

In recent years an extremely large number of off-shore trusts have been set up. These usually contain the so-called "Cuba clause," which allows the *situs* and proper law of the trust to be transferred from one jurisdiction to another.

Business Trusts

In essence, a trust offers a means by which funds can be "settled" for the future benefit of specified beneficiaries. The actual management of the trust is usually handed over to one or more professional trustees, and the trust deed can specify that they may use their discretion to periodically distribute the trust funds to the beneficiaries prescribed in the original deed. Clearly, it is to the advantage of all concerned for a trust fund to be established in a low-tax or tax free area rather than in the high-tax jurisdiction of the settlor. In this way, the trust fund investments can accumulate at a preferential tax rate. An alternative, of course, is for an individual to set up a private investment holding company off-shore over which he exercises control by means of a beneficially owned shareholdings.

Trust law is found in both the common law and in the civil law systems, and there are significant differences between them. The former are prevalent in havens that are or were British territories, such as the Cayman Islands, the Bahamas, Bermuda, Hong Kong, or the Isle of Man. The latter are found in havens, with a civil law tradition, such as Liechtenstein, Switzerland, and Panama.

An effective method of hiding the ownership of an underlying company is to interpose a discretionary trust between the beneficial owners and the underlying companies. A discretionary trust is one created under Anglo-Saxon law in which the classes of beneficiaries are named in the trust documents but their remuneration is dependent on the exercise of the sole discretion of the trustees. Under general trust law, beneficiaries of discretionary

Figure 3.4. Using a trust to conceal beneficial ownership.

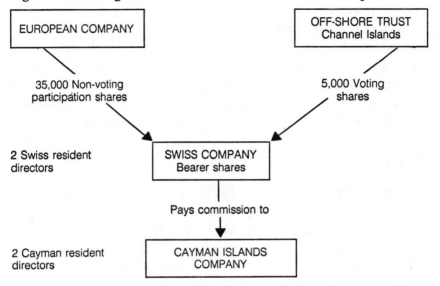

trusts are not the owners of the trusts or their assets or income. If the overall ownership of the trading companies is vested in the trustees, the directors of those underlying companies may be able to identify the trusts as owners of the companies truthfully without involving the beneficial owners. The actual beneficiaries of the trust would be known only to the trustees in a tax haven jurisdiction.

A plan benefiting from the involvement of a tax haven and trust is illustrated in Figure 3.4 in which a European group exports commodity X to Japan and the United States. Because Japan and the United States impose a quota for the import of commodity X from the European country (i.e., Portugal and Spain), it is considered necessary to route commodity X through a company resident in a third country.

As a beneficiary of a nondiscretionary trust is not viewed as the owner of the trust, it is possible for a company that is such a beneficiary to utilize the trust. Thus, in order to own a variety of subsidiaries located in several countries so as to route the commodity/product

) the jurisdiction which institutes a quota system for imported products.

Under general company law, a company is controlled by its voting shareholders. In Figure 3.4, the voting shares in the Swiss company are owned by the trustees, who are not from the specific
European country (i.e., Portugal and Spain) residents. Provided the
trustees are resident in a low-tax area, such as the Cayman Islands or
the Channel Islands, there will be no tax consequences.

Reliance on Trusts

For many years foreign trusts have been a popular mechanism in estate planning throughout the world, particularly in the United States
and Europe. Certain property may be transferred free of taxes to foreign trusts. In some instances where there is a tax on the property,
the assets can be transferred to a foreign trust at a rate lower than the
capital gains rate that would be levied if the property was sold.

The United States has taken various measures to ensure the security of trusts established in foreign countries to minimize the risk of
adverse changes in foreign law that might be enforced to the detri-
ment of the trust or corporate assets. For example, in the context of
foreign trusts, trust provisions purporting to effect an automatic conversion of the trust into a trust of Country Y with a trustee in Country
Y in the event of detrimental changes in the law of Country X have
been used. In the corporate context, arrangements for a transfer of
corporate assets to a trustee for the benefit of the shareholders in the
event of an adverse change in the law of Country X have occasionally
been used.

For foreign trusts founded by U.S. persons, it is important to
choose a jurisdiction that recognizes the Anglo-American system of
common law to accord the trust all the legal attributes of U.S. law.
This precludes Switzerland and Liechtenstein, where a *Stiftung* is
the entity used as a trust, and Panama and the Netherlands Antilles, where property rights are interpreted differently from common
law rules. However, the Cayman Islands, with its exempt trust permitted to exist for 100 years and 50 years of guaranteed tax exemp-

tion as well as a regulatory environment, is a preferable site for foreign law trusts.

As a result of the increasing interest in foreign trusts in which assets are held by a custodian outside the United States, the double trust (a trust that owns another trust) has been used by certain management investing or servicing organizations. However, in order to eliminate abusive tax shelters, the IRS now scrutinizes all canceled checks, statements, invoices, travel records, and other pertinent documents that may indicate the use of double trusts or foreign connections related to them. If two trusts are used, it is extremely important to make certain that a U.S. trust is not used as the second trust, but that both trusts are foreign trusts, each in a different country. It is also necessary to ensure that there is no U.S. beneficiary, trustee, or creator in the entire structure.

One use for the double trust vehicle considered by certain British banks is a Cayman trust for the first trust and a U.K. trust for the second. In the event that this method is practiced, the settlor of the trust may not be domiciled in the United Kingdom, so that any capital gains made by the trust will not be liable to U.K. tax. Moreover, this trust would not be subject to the U.K. capital transfer tax if it does not hold any assets in the United Kingdom. If the trustees of the U.K. trust are under obligation to pay the income to the Panamanian trust and the income is not U.K.-source income, then no U.K. tax will be levied. It is preferable for the U.K. trust to open a bank account in a third country, such as Luxembourg or Switzerland, and to arrange for all the income to be transferred to that account.

To avoid or reduce the 30% withholding tax on investments made in the United States through the trust, the U.K. trust would channel its investments through an underlying subsidiary in a third country having a tax treaty with the United States. This means that the U.K. trust would hold the assets and could have capital gains free of tax, but then would loan the proceeds of the tax-free sale to a third country with a tax treaty with the United States, such as Luxembourg, where a Luxembourg resident company other than a holding company could be the vehicle for the investment in the United States. A third country is preferred because under the U.K.-U.S. Income Tax Convention there would be a "fiscal residence" as defined in the treaty, since the U.K. trust would not be subjected to the U.K. tax on U.S. source income as long as the income was paid into the Cayman trust. By establishing the Luxembourg resident company as the depository of funds, the interest would be remitted free of tax from the United States to Luxembourg under the treaty between the two countries and, under Luxembourg domestic law, there would be no withholding tax paid on interest paid by the Luxembourg company to the U.K. trust.

The United States is at present most sensitive to the use of the Caribbean area by resident U.S. companies. In its official report entitled "Crime and Secrecy: the Use of Off-shore Banks and Companies," the IRS emphasized the increasing importance of tax havens. It pointed out that in 1985 there were 36,000 off-shore companies in the Cayman Islands, of which 30 were multinational commercial banks and 300 were "brass plate" banks, while the population of the country was only approximately 17,000. The 1986 Tax Reform Act attempted to take measures prohibiting the switching of income from one country to another in order to maximize foreign tax credits (see U.S. Tax Aspects section).

TREATY SHOPPING

There are two main ways in which treaty shopping occurs:

 Direct-conduit method; and

 Stepping-stone method.

Direct-Conduit Method. The direct-conduit method of treaty shopping is illustrated in Figure 3.5. In this example, the tax treaty between Country A and Country B provides for an exemption from Country A's tax on dividends paid by companies in Country A to shareholders in Country B. Country C has no tax treaty with either Country A or B. In order to benefit from the dividend exemption in the A-B tax treaty, a company resident in Country C establishes a wholly owned subsidiary in Country A.

Figure 3.5. Treaty shopping: direct-conduit method.

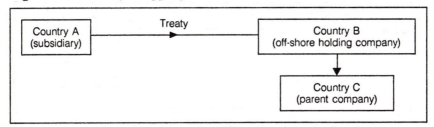

The Country C parent then transfers all its shares in the Country A company to another wholly owned subsidiary in Country B. This intermediary company is exempt under Country B's domestic law on dividends received from a wholly owned subsidiary. The income from the parent company's investment in Country A can thus be accumulated tax-free in Country B. The same sort of result might be achieved if Country B was a tax haven. Thus, the success of the conduit method depends on the intermediary company being located in a low tax jurisdiction.

Stepping-Stone Method.   The stepping-stone method of treaty shopping is illustrated in Figure 3.6. In this example, the tax treaty between Country A and Country B provides for an exemption from Country A's tax for interest going from Country A to residents of Country B. Country C has no tax treaty with either Country A or B. In order to benefit from this provision in the A-B treaty, a company in Country C assigns to a subsidiary in Country B the loans it has made to persons resident in Country A. The subsidiary in Country B, in order to provide the consideration for this assignment, borrows an equivalent amount at an equivalent rate of interest from the parent company. The subsidiary is liable in principle to Country B's tax on the interest it receives, but the liability is effectively eliminated because the subsidiary's taxable income is reduced to nil by a deduction for the interest that it has to pay. Country B does not impose a withholding tax on interest, and the parent company is exempt from domestic tax on the income in its own country of residence. Thus, the parent company uses the A-B treaty as a stepping-stone to enable it to receive its interest from Country B without suffering Country B's tax.

Figure 3.6. Treaty shopping: stepping-stone method.

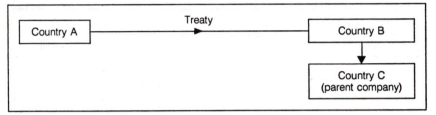

The essential difference between the direct-conduit method and the stepping-stone method is that the direct-conduit method makes use of an exemption from tax in the intermediary country while the stepping-stone method reduces a tax liability in that country by a counterbalancing expense.

An intermediary company may not always be necessary. Sometimes a partnership or trust will serve as well or better as a tax-free conduit for funds. Furthermore, the income involved may change its nature or character at different stages in the process. For example, a company in Country B receiving interest from Country A may, if it is advantageous to do so, transfer the interest to a parent company in a third country in the form of a dividend.

Techniques for Emigrants and Retirees

Emigration often provides an individual with the ideal opportunity to use tax havens for international tax planning. One of the most effective techniques stems from the fact that, while on his journey to his new home, the emigrant is "in limbo" and not subject to any particular fiscal system. This fact allows him to engage in "island hopping," whereby he breaks his journey by visiting a tax haven and invests a portion of his assets there. The effect of this is to avoid future taxation on the income from those assets if the country of his destination taxes income based on source. In this case, the source of the income would be the tax haven and, even upon receipt of such income, tax is unlikely to be levied.

The principal of "island hopping" can be combined with the use of a trust in order to avoid estate duty. By transferring assets to a trust formed in a tax haven, ownership of the assets ceases to vest in the individual. The immediate result is that the income generated by those assets no longer accrues to their former owner. The longer term advantage is that the assets no longer form part of the emigrant's estate, and upon his death no estate duty will be payable on them. The transferring of assets can be a complicated transaction, and great care must be taken in the drawing of the necessary trust deed.

When moving from one country to another, the factor of domicile becomes important in international tax planning. An individual's domicile is the country that he regards as his permanent home. Thus, if he becomes resident in a new country, but still retains the intention of returning to his previous home at a later date, his domicile will not coincide with his residence. Movement from one country to another, even for a relatively long "temporary" absence, is unlikely to change an individual's domicile. This factor may be of prime importance because certain fiscal systems levy tax on the basis of domicile, granting persons who are resident but not domiciled in that country certain tax concessions.

Domicile.   The United Kingdom is a prime example where tax benefits arise when one's domicile and residence do not coincide. The main advantage of using a U.K. domicile is that the individual concerned will then cease to be liable to U.K. inheritance tax on non-U.K. assets. A non-resident but U.K.-domiciled individual remains liable to U.K. inheritance tax on his worldwide assets. The opportunity to use a tax haven exists when an individual leaves the United Kingdom to work abroad permanently and thus cease to be U.K. domiciled—by setting up a trust in the Channel Islands for all his non-U.K. sited assets.

An interesting situation arises from different definitions of corporate residence given by the United States and the United Kingdom. The U.S. tax code states that a company is resident if it is incorporated in the United States. For the British, residency is wherever management and control lies. The opportunity exists to set up a dual residence subsidiary that is incorporated in the United States, but operated in the United Kingdom. This enables the parent corporation to claim the same losses or deductions to offset profits and thereby reduce taxes in both countries simultaneously.

The Channel Islands are a location used by many people who wish to retire in Britain. Such an individual can set up an off-shore discretionary trust in the Channel Islands, ensuring that he will be the beneficiary of the trust during his lifetime, so that he will obtain an income from the trust.

4

The Benefits of Tax
Haven Operations

BUSINESS OTHER THAN MULTINATIONALS

It is clearly possible for all U.S. exporters to take advantage of low-tax countries/tax havens in order to lower their distribution costs as well as reduce import charges of their product. Currently, many U.S. exporters are preoccupied with the concept of entering Europe through countries that offer low transaction costs. The newly established processing center and tax haven, Madeira, is a prime example of a jurisdiction that can provide generous benefits to U.S. exporters by offering extremely low customs and import duties to manufacturers transferring and processing merchandise through its free-trade zone and onto Europe via Portugal's European Community status.

WHO USES A TAX HAVEN

The importance of tax havens has grown in step with the growth of multinational companies and their increased reliance on the benefits of tax havens in the day-to-day operation of their worldwide businesses.

Tax havens have a strong appeal for multinational corporations organized in foreign countries because of the advantages they offer for timate avoidance or deferment of taxation on certain profits earned overseas. Profits harbored in a tax sanctuary enable working capital to be used in its cheapest form.

Traditionally, a tax haven is used as a central point for handling paperwork and preparing and processing trade documents. Many companies utilize on tax havens for the passage of title of goods, so that these transfers may take place without undue regulations. Tax havens are also used as off-shore centers to administer patent and trademark royalty agreements. Because of the intangible characteristics of patents and royalties, these assets can be moved from one location to another that is more convenient to the owner.

If a company with branches and subsidiaries abroad is a resident of a country with strict foreign exchange regulations, it may not wish to take the profits earned overseas to its home country because it later may have difficulty reinvesting them abroad. To avoid this, it may establish a foreign intermediate holding company in a tax haven, not primarily for tax reasons but to avoid the obstacle of foreign exchange control.

Additional benefits of tax havens include:

- Secrecy for foreign bank accounts and privacy for ownership and financial records;
- Procedures for shifting investments without tax;
- A minimum of government regulations and control;
- Asset diversification and asset protection;
- Convenient geographic location;
- Liberal processes for capital formation and registration;
- Adaptability to the requirements of individuals and investment syndicates; and
- Flexible provisions for inheritance.

It should be noted that in many cases the interposition of an intermediate holding company does not result in a definite avoidance of tax, but rather in tax deferral. Sooner or later, the parent company must receive the accumulated income, which is then taxable, possibly without a credit for foreign taxes paid in previous years in the country from which the income was originally derived. It should also be noted that most tax havens lack tax treaties with major economic powers and as such the use of a tax haven country often prevents the beneficiary of the income from benefiting from reduced withholding rates that otherwise might have become available under a tax treaty.

To appreciate how using a tax haven intermediary can achieve different goals in the same business arrangement, consider the structure illustrated in Figure 4.1. Company P, located in Country C, owns a patent. It receives a considerable amount of annual royalty income from an independent company, R, located in Country D. There is no tax treaty between Countries C and D. The royalties are subject to a 25% withholding tax in Country D and a 50% tax on the remainder in Country C, making the total tax burden 62.5%. To avoid this tax, Company P creates a patent holding company, S, in tax haven Country E, which has concluded tax treaties with both C and D. Under the D-E treaty, the royalties paid to Company S are no longer taxed in Country D. Company S pays a 5% tax in Country E on the royalties it receives, which constitute its profit. It distributes the remainder to Company P as dividends, after withholding 5% of that amount under the C-E treaty. Since Company P is exempt from tax on dividends received from its subsidiary in Country E under the C-E treaty, the total tax burden on the royalties has been reduced to less than 10%, with no apparent business purpose other than the avoidance of tax.

Now consider that the same Company P has licensed its patent to the same Company R. Company R intends to use the patent in a large factory project in a third country for which price conditions have already been fixed. The price conditions are such that Company R will be able to pay no more than a modest royalty. With a tax burden of 62.5%, Company P will not be able to meet its current expenses for the license. However, by creating the tax haven subsidiary in Country E and reducing the total tax burden, Company P can make the project viable. In this case, in addition to a significant tax

Figure 4.1. Patent royalties paid through a tax haven.

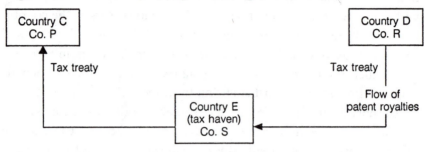

saving, there is also a sound financial reason for what otherwise would be an artificial structure.

TAKING ADVANTAGE OF BANKING SERVICES

It is often be worthwhile for a multinational company to establish a subsidiary in a tax haven and endowing it with a generous bank account. This subsidiary is then able to lend money to another foreign subsidiary after opening a time-deposit account, which serves as collateral. Interest earned on the time-deposit account in the tax haven accrues free of tax. In many locations, the borrower's expense for interest will qualify as a tax deduction.

The potential investor should be aware that off-shore banking can invite scrutiny by national tax authorities. Medium-sized banks have decided to establish branches in tax havens to expand their international loan portfolios if the volume of their transactions is not large enough to warrant a full branch in a major center such as London.

Most of the world's major international banks and many multinational companies have set up off-shore operations in tax havens to cope with Eurodollar operations or to deal with foreign trust business. In an increasing number of cases, these off-shore banks are established as "captives." The enactment of strict legislation governing the conduct and integrity of these banks has largely eliminated the incorporation of shell banks. Although shells can still be incorporated in St Vincent the more established locations of off-shore banking, such as Switzerland, Luxembourg, the Bahamas, the Cayman Islands, and the Netherlands Antilles, all insist on "reasonable banking standards" before they will issue licenses. Tight regulations are also found in havens newly established, such as Nauru, the New Hebrides, and Turks and Caicos. The Channel Islands of Jersey and Guernsey not only exercise strict controls, but have restricted the opening of new banks. It is clear, therefore, that an individual or company dealing with a tax haven bank can be reassured—particularly in the case of a subsidiary of a large international bank—that he will be in good hands.

OFF-SHORE HOLDING COMPANIES

In the context of an international group of companies, the parent company may choose to incorporate an off-shore holding company to own a foreign subsidiary. The holding company might be located in one of a number of jurisdictions, such as the Netherlands, Switzerland, and Luxembourg, that grant special tax privileges to holding companies. An off-shore holding company may provide some or all of the following benefits:

■ Reduced withholding taxes—By establishing a holding company that benefits a tax treaty with the country in which the foreign subsidiary is established; dividend interest and royalty payments may flow more freely of withholding tax from the foreign subsidiary's country.

■ Tax deferral dividends—Under the tax laws of the parent's home country, dividends received from the foreign subsidiary may be fully taxed at home. By interposing an off-shore holding company, tax on such dividends can be deferred, since the dividends will be received by the holding company rather than by the home company. The holding company is able to accumulate the profits of the various subsidiaries, reinvest those profits in other overseas projects while avoiding taxes on the projects if they were distributed to the parent's home country.

■ Mix of foreign taxes—If the parent's home country taxes dividends received from foreign subsidiaries, it will normally give foreign tax credits for the taxes paid by the foreign subsidiaries. By placing all foreign subsidiaries under one off-shore holding company, these tax credits can be mixed so that high and low rates of taxes are combined in order to create an optimum tax credit fewer excess credits wasted.

■ Tax deferral on capital gains—The home-country parent can defer home-country capital gains tax on the sale of a foreign subsidiary by placing ownership in an off-shore holding company. On the sale of the subsidiary, the holding company will pay no capital gains tax (as no capital gains tax is levied in the off-shore jurisdiction—ultimately will pay U.S. capital gains tax, but benefit of deferral).

■ Freedom from exchange control—Where the home country imposes exchange controls on foreign investments, the formation of an off-shore holding company enables the parent company to continue making foreign investments by repatriating the profits of the foreign subsidiaries only as far as the off-shore holding company.

REAL ESTATE

A private investor in real estate could benefit by establishing an off-shore company to hold his real estate investment. This is permitted in most havens, although Luxembourg is a notable exception. Such ownership has the advantage of preserving a degree of anonymity in the owner. It also offers the possibility of limiting eventual capital gains tax liability by the expedient of selling shares in the company that owns the real estate rather than selling the property itself. Depending on the haven selected, it is usually possible to invest in local real estate.

Significant corporate ownership of foreign real estate exists. For U.S. corporations that control plants, factories, hotels, or office buildings worldwide, it is often possible to set up an intermediary company or trust to handle the management affairs of the properties, particularly where these properties are located in high-tax jurisdictions. If the intermediary company's/trust's management can be shown to operate and manage the properties—a significant amount of pre-tax profits can be transferred through management fees to the tax haven, thereby reducing any excess foreign tax credits. In addition, when the properties are sold, capital gains tax in the high-tax jurisdiction may be deferred if the ownership is registered in the tax haven and the ultimate capital gains will be paid in the United States after the benefits of deferral.

The benefits of foreigners managing and owning U.S. real estate through off-shore jurisdictions as against a local subsidiary is clear when reviewing the tax legislation of branch profits. Through direct ownership from an off-shore source, foreign corporations are able to reduce U.S. tax costs. Off-shore trusts or corporations can be utilized to maximum benefit. As mentioned earlier, Orient-Express the hotel and train operator has utilized tax haven trusts to control a variety of its European hotels.

OFF-SHORE LICENSING AND PATENT-HOLDING COMPANIES

Royalties paid under license for patents or other intangible rights can be effectively sheltered from taxation by using an off-shore licensing company. Collateral benefits can be gained, as well.

For example, the owner of a patent can create an off-shore licensing company and assign the patent to the off-shore company, intending that the off-shore company will license rights in the patent to a foreign subsidiary. By having the royalties paid to the licensing company in a tax haven, profits are effectively shifted from the foreign subsidiary to the off-shore patent-owning company, which pays little or no tax on the royalties received. Income from other intangible rights, such as trademarks, copyrights, know-how, and franchising rights, can be earned without incurring withholding or income tax if a tax haven company is established to sublicense other companies in various countries.

A tax saving can also be achieved on patent royalties by combining tax havens. The United States does not deduct withholding tax on royalties paid to a Dutch company. Thus, if a tax haven company in the Netherlands Antilles sets up a Dutch subsidiary, and licenses its patents to the Dutch company, the Dutch company, in turn, can license to an American manufacturer. The American company can then pay the Dutch subsidiary the patent royalties free of tax. The Dutch company can pay the royalty to the tax haven company (the patent owner), thereby avoiding Dutch withholding taxes on dividends. The Dutch company is not taxed in the Netherlands, and the tax haven company avoids the U.S. 30% withholding tax.

It is possible to use a network of tax treaties and havens to obtain the best features of each in order to avoid on-shore withholding taxes. This is illustrated in Figure 4.2, which demonstrates how a German patentee can license a U.S. corporation without paying either German or U.S. tax. In this example, the German patentee assigns the patent to a Liechtenstein holding company. It grants a license to a Swiss letter-box company, which in turn licenses the U.S. corporation. The U.S. corporation pays royalties to the Swiss company that are free of U.S. withholding tax by virtue of the U.S.-Swiss tax treaty. The Swiss company pays a royalty to the Liechtenstein company equal in amount to the royalty received from the U.S. corporation, thereby avoiding all liabilities for withholding tax or profits tax. The Liechtenstein company pays no profits tax or tax on the distribution of profits, and the royalties are accumulated until they are required by the German patentee. As a further incentive, if the German patentee owns the U.S. corporation and ensures that the royalty rate is high, the German patentee will also absorb a significant amount of the U.S. profit (Horwarth & Horwarth).

OFF-SHORE FINANCE COMPANIES

A multinational group can use an off-shore finance company to channel loans to a foreign subsidiary. By routing interest to the off-shore finance company, profits are effectively shifted from the foreign subsidiary to the off-shore company, which pays little or no tax on the

Figure 4.2. Patent licensing to shelter royalties.

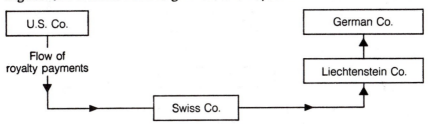

interest received. It may be necessary for the loans to be channeled through a variety of companies in order to avoid or reduce withholding taxes arising from dividends and interest paid from the foreign subsidiary. A typical lending system is illustrated in Figure 4.3.

The off-shore finance company is often utilized to raise outside borrowings for the group as a whole. Its attraction to lenders will be that it can pay them interest free of withholding tax deductions, since invariably it will be located in a territory that imposes no withholding taxes at the source. Figure 4.4 illustrates how an entire group of companies can be funded from a tax haven and thus obtain low-cost financing and minimize taxation.

It is important to note that much anti-avoidance legislation prevents the tax-efficient use of interposing finance companies between the subsidiaries of a multinational group. For example, it is maintained by the United States that, if subsidiary A lends to or finances subsidiaries B and C, this amounts to a dividend from A to the other subsidiaries. However, if a separate finance subsidiary company is placed beneath the subsidiaries to be financed, as is illustrated in Fig-

Figure 4.3. Structure using off-shore finance company.

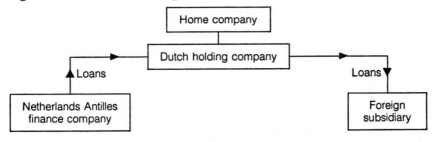

Figure 4.4. Sample group of companies funded from a tax haven.

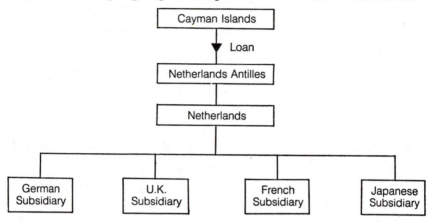

ure 4.5, the U.S. anti-avoidance legislation is nullified as the finance subsidiary will lend separately to each subsidiary to be funded.

Through the use of the Dutch participation, exemption dividends from the underlying subsidiaries will flow onto the Netherlands Antilles (after 5% Dutch tax) where the maximum rate of tax, 7.5%, will be drastically reduced as a result of interest paid to the Cayman Islands' financing company. By interposing a Netherlands finance company between the payer company and a separate off-shore company, as illustrated in Figure 4.6 by the dotted lines, the group can exploit the tax treaties entered into by the Netherlands to avoid withholding taxes that might be due to either the United States (30%), the United Kingdom (25%), Germany (25%), or France (33⅓%). The interest payment thus originating from the United States can pass on

Figure 4.5. Structure using finance subsidiary company.

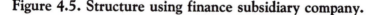
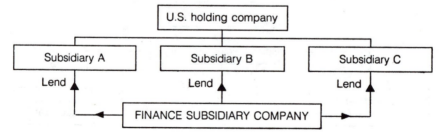

Figure 4.6. Structure interposing a Netherlands finance company.

to the Netherlands company at 0% withholding tax and to the off-shore company after a minimal tax deduction.

It is interesting to note that the entire Dutch tax charge can be avoided by utilizing a Belgian branch owned by the Netherlands finance company, as illustrated in Figure 4.6 by the solid lines. The branch would receive the interest payments subject to no withholding tax as a result of making use of its Dutch parent's treaty network. If the Belgian branch then chose to remit these interest receipts to an off-shore company in the form of management fees, no tax at all would be paid. The structure using the Belgian branch is shielded from the Dutch tax of 0.125% under the Dutch law that provides that a Dutch parent need not pay tax where it has set up a foreign branch.

Conduit Finance Companies

A conduit finance company is of prime benefit where it receives interest subject to the minimum possible rates of withholding tax under applicable double-taxation treaties. Thereafter, it pays most of this interest on to another territory. The interest payment represents a tax deductible expense, but there remains a small margin that will be subject to full corporate taxes in the territory where the conduit finance company is established. A suitable location for a conduit finance company will therefore require the following characteristics:

- An extensive network of favorable double-taxation treaties;
- No/low withholding tax on interest payments; and
- Corporate tax rules allowing the full deductibility of interest expense paid to non-residents with the requirement of keeping a small margin in the conduit finance company.

Thus, for example, a conduit finance company may lend funds at 9½% and receive the interest subject to No/low withholding taxes as a result of the benefit of double-taxation treaties between the country of residence of the borrowers, and pay interest at a rate of 9% on an equivalent loan from a company in another territory. The conduit finance company would thus earn a ½% margin. This spread would normally be subject to corporate taxes in the country where the conduit finance company is located and represents the "cost" of taking advantage of favorable tax treaties.

The Netherlands is the prime location for conduit finance companies. Its wide network of double-taxation treaties provides favorable relief from withholding tax on interest.

The Netherlands also has the major advantage of imposing no withholding taxes at all on interest payments by a Netherlands company, wherever the recipient is located. Thus, a Netherlands finance company can pay interest directly to a tax haven without any Dutch withholding tax being incurred.

Interest payments to a Netherlands company are fully deductible for corporate income tax purposes, provided that they are at an arm's length rate and there are normally no debt-to-equity restrictions for finance companies.

The final advantage of the Netherlands for conduit finance companies is that the Dutch tax authorities are normally prepared to give rulings as to what interest margin they will regard as arm's length in a particular situation. The expected interest margins are normally between ⅛% and ⅟₁₆% for inter-group loans and ¼% to ⅟₃₂% for loans outside the group.

Finance Company in Zero- or Low-Tax Jurisdiction

This finance company will normally be unable to enjoy useful double-taxation treaties to minimize withholding taxes on interest. However, it will be able to accumulate interest income without subjecting it to higher corporate taxes that might apply in the country where a conduit finance company is established.

Figure 4.7. Dual finance company structure.

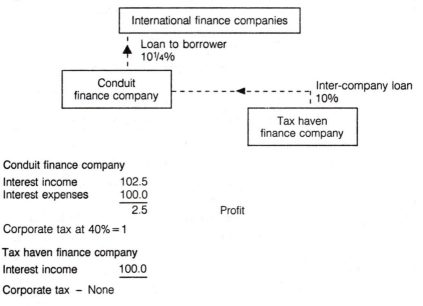

Conduit finance company

Interest income	102.5
Interest expenses	100.0
	2.5

Corporate tax at 40% = 1

Tax haven finance company

Interest income	100.0

Corporate tax – None

Dual Finance Company

It is often advantageous to establish a conduit finance company together with a finance company located in a tax haven. This facilitates
the minimization of withholding tax on interest and to accumulate
interest income subject to minimal taxes. Such a structure is illustrated in Figure 4.7, where the conduct finance company borrows
$1,000 from the tax haven finance company.

BORROWING FINANCE COMPANIES

A borrowing finance company could be used where a parent company
wished to borrow funds from a company located in a territory that had
no double-taxation treaty with the parent company's jurisdiction. If
the parent company's jurisdiction would impose a significant withholding tax on interest payments to non-residents, the lender might
insist on increasing the interest rate to account for the withholding

Figure 4.8. U.K. parent company borrowing on a back-to-back basis.

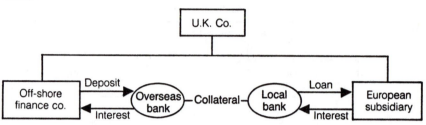

tax that would be suffered. This is especially the case where the lender is located in a territory where there is no effective double-taxation relief for foreign withholding taxes.

An example of this dilemma would be a loan to a U.K. holding company from a bank in Hong Kong, which has no tax treaties with the United Kingdom. If the Hong Kong bank had no U.K. branch, U.K. withholding tax at the current basic income tax rate of 25% would apply to interest payments to the bank. Since no effective double-taxation relief would normally be available for such withholding tax, the bank would most likely require that the interest coupon be increased by the withholding tax, thus limiting any economic advantage to undertake borrowing.

The trading subsidiaries of the U.K. parent company could borrow from a bank on a back-to-back basis against the collateral of a deposit made by an off-shore finance company.

For maximum tax savings, the finance company should be located in a country in which the group intends to expand. Thus, lending more credibility to the structure.

DOUBLE-INTEREST-DEDUCTION COMPANIES

In certain circumstances, international finance companies may effectively achieve a double interest deduction for a group by using complex structures.

Such a structure is illustrated in Figure 4.9. In this structure the parent company of the multinational group borrows funds that are injected into a finance company in a tax haven. This company then

Figure 4.9. Double-interest-deduction structure.

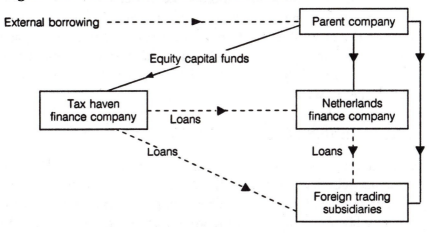

lends the funds at a market interest rate to group subsidiaries in other countries. This lending is often routed via a conduit finance company located in a territory such as the Netherlands to take advantage of its double-taxation treaties. Such a structure can achieve an effective double deduction of interest both in the parent company and in the subsidiary locations, while ensuring that the interest from the subsidiaries flows into the tax haven.

Anti-avoidance legislation problems can best be avoided if the proposed off-shore companies have a real commercial presence in their country of operation and residence. In order to establish a commercial presence, the off-shore company would need to establish its own premises and employ its own staff in the territory concerned. It would also greatly help an off-shore finance company if it received income from its parent. Therefore such companies may have to wait until a group expands overseas, establishing subsidiaries in many different locations.

CAPTIVE BANKS

The term "captive bank" is used to refer to a banking subsidiary set up in a tax haven or financial center to operate principally for the benefit of the members of a multinational group and their customers and suppliers. Captive banks may also operate as merchant banks and offer in-house commercial banking and financing services. Thus, through the establishment of an in-house bank, currency swaps and other transactions can be concluded without service fees. These transactions are often concluded in less time than they would be by an external bank.

CAPTIVE INSURANCE COMPANIES

A captive insurance company is a wholly or jointly owned foreign insurance subsidiary incorporated in a tax haven in which there is no tax or a minimum of tax on income from premiums or reinvestments generated by the insurance of the worldwide risks of the parent company. Premiums paid to captive insurance companies are often tax deductible. Some high-tax jurisdictions have incorporated measures against captive insurance companies into their anti-avoidance provisions. However, they have not extended these provisions to cover reinsurance companies, which clearly can also be established as wholly owned subsidiaries in an appropriate tax haven.

The inducements for establishing an insurance subsidiary include:

- Lower insurance costs achieved by eliminating marketing and sales costs and commissions; substantial savings also can be achieved because the premiums do not reflect a built in profit margin;

- Increased liquidity, because premiums are available for investment by the parent or associated companies, not paid in advance to a commercial insurance company;

- Ability to get insurance coverage on risks not normally insured by commercial sources, such as nuclear risk, supertankers, and labor strikes;

- Superior coverage terms by writing a policy to suit the needs of the group. A captive insurance company is paid premiums to insure risks around an international group and then reinsures those risks in the market. Reinsurance is usually also cheaper than insurance. Over a period of time the captive gradually invests and uses those reserves to cease to reinsure until, assuming no claims are made over and above what is expected, a large sum of money will accrue overseas. On a worldwide basis the payment of a premium to a captive allows the various companies in the group around the world to obtain tax relief.

The United States has taken specific anti-tax-avoidance measures. U.S.-owned captives established outside the United States are classified as controlled foreign corporations and achieve no tax savings unless:

- A foreign corporation owns at least 50% of the captive and U.S. risks are limited to 75% of the insured total; or
- A foreign corporation owns at least 75% of the captive.

Less than 20% of the foreign corporation's gross insurance receipts may come from a "U.S. related person." Because of this, many captives are established as joint ventures.

SHIPPING COMPANIES

A ship service or an aircraft service that engages in international activity may choose to establish a tax haven company to minimize or completely avoid taxes. Many tax havens are flag-of-convenience nations. These allow foreign ship owners to register under the tax haven flag to avoid taxes and the economic restrictions and frequently onerous rules and regulations of their own nations. For example, American ship owners have traditionally registered their vessels under the flags of Liberia or Panama. By flying a flag of convenience, these owners have been able to avoid the extensive U.S. regulations that govern the size and qualifications of crews, minimum wages, safety equipment, and pollution control. In addition to the traditional shipping havens of Liberia and Panama, the Bahamas, Bermuda, the Cayman Islands, Cyprus, Hong Kong, and the Isle of Man all offer inducements that should attract a portion of this market.

TOURISM COMPANIES

The travel business is well-suited for exploiting the benefits of tax havens. For example, a retailer or group of retailers could make a viable operation out of establishing its own travel wholesale operation in a tax haven such as Bermuda and channelling its European business through it.

It is important to understand that the tax-free profits of such a Bermuda-based operation should not be repatriated to the United States, where they would be subject to taxation. Instead, these profits should be invested in other foreign operations where capital growth can continue unhampered. Hotel construction or operation is an excellent vehicle for reinvestment, particularly in one of the many tax haven jurisdictions, such as Puerto Rico, that offer tax holidays of from five to 30 years to companies that construct or otherwise invest in hotels. The well-known travel company Orient Express utilizes Bermuda for its holding company and owns hotels in Europe through trusts established in European tax havens.

5

Role of Tax Havens in International Finance

Financial regulation in any form encourages avoidance and stimulates the creation of an alternative international trading system. This stimulation is especially strong for invisible trade activities in low-tax or zero-tax off-shore centers. An example of this effect is the creation of the Eurocurrency centers, both on-shore and off-shore, which have furnished a transnational financial resource of common property for companies, individuals, and governments. Likewise, the burgeoning Eurobond market has encouraged the development of jurisdictions that offer generous fiscal and company legislation, particularly those that impose no withholding tax on interest or dividends, irrespective of the residence of the bondholder.

Many tax havens have developed further by participating in the internationalization of money and credit markets that followed the creation of the Interbank Markets and the Eurocurrency and Eurobond Markets in the 1960s and the general spread of transnational banking in the 1970s. These developments were encouraged by the electronic revolution in fund transfer, which considerably reduced the costs and inconvenience of operating banks in remote locations and made business activity between time zones viable. This gave rise to international wholesale banking, in which large-denomination deposits in a variety of currencies are obtained via extensive world-wide branch networks from non-resident corporate customers, banks, and government agencies and are re-lent transnationally through such markets to similar sectors. These deposit-gathering, loan-distributing, network infrastructures also made possible the diversification of new transnational business superstructures, as well as the practice of international sub-contracting via syndicated loan activities.

An example of this network structure is the U.S. holding company Citicorp. In 1981 Citicorp had 33 domestic subsidiaries. Off-shore, of 73 international subsidiaries, 18 were located in 12 separate tax haven centers. Of 17 international affiliates, 4 were located in 2 tax havens. Its overseas branches were located in 80 countries, 17 of which were tax haven centers. Chase Manhattan Bank and Republic National Bank of New York have extensive networks of subsidiaries in most well-known tax havens around the world. Many of these companies located in the tax havens operated as finance subsidiaries, they are often able to obtain a far lower cost of capital for the parent then the parent company could achieve directly. Higher profits are often possible through the tax haven companies, as a result of less stringent regulations that facilitate more bank lending and higher leverage, as a percentage of market capitalization.

Whatever factors influenced the development of the individual tax havens, all of these centers have become production interfaces linked to, yet separate from, on-shore world capital markets and invisible production centers. The establishment of a network of such centers, whether based on the Euromarkets or transnational banking, has constituted a new secondary trading system that is global in scope, unlike the largely intra-continental system that preceded it. As economies of convenience, these off-shore havens have provided an international common property resource for transnational private-sector business in at least five basic respects:

■ As centers of domicile through which international companies can incorporate and operate commercial holding companies and overseas subsidiaries in the most advantageous fiscal climate subject to minimal exchange control.

■ As holding companies, which are used predominantly to control industrial or investment companies by holding major shares, to finance companies in a group by generating funds through the flotation of bond issues, and, not least, to receive dividends, interest, or royalty and licensing payments.

■ As locations from and through which to exploit international capital and money markets with a greater freedom of action than might be feasible from their countries of origin. Eurobonds created an urgent need for the services of countries with favorable tax legislation, such as an absence of withholding tax on interest and dividends, regardless of the bondholder's residence. Because Eurobonds are bearer securities that protect the anonymity of the holder, this is particularly important for the growing category of Eurobond investors who have taken care to arrange their affairs so that they escape liability to tax anywhere.

■ As secure havens for international earnings, savings, and pools of liquidity for investment in a tax-neutral environment.

■ As assembly centers for components produced externally in on-shore centers and re-exported on-shore, through free trade zones (R. A. Johns).

Globally there are two separate types of effects theoretically consequent to the establishment of intermediate economies (tax haven economies that create an effect of on-shore money flows leaving these high tax on-shore areas) orientated essentially to invisible trade that involves on-shore industrial "slippage" (i.e., off-shore movement of manufacturing activities and capital for investments in real estate and exports) and an erosion of actual or potential tax bases:

■ Invisible trade diversion, where the overseas trade or investment activity merely uses the off-shore haven as a routing or "paper" center, where institutions located elsewhere merely have a "brass plate" or "shell" existence. In this case, the haven seeks merely to attract income leakages from the economies in which its clients are based, and little real financial development takes place with respect to international banking.

- ■ Invisible trade creation, where the trade or investment activity uses the off-shore center as a "functional" center where deposit-taking, final lending, and financial intermediation is actually carried out. Off-shore subsidiary or branch business will tend to involve wholesale operations, so that access to and standing in the local or nearest Interbank market will be important for liquidity management and matching of the types and maturities of assets and liabilities.

OFF-SHORE INVESTMENT FUNDS

Off-shore funds are understood to include any mutual investment fund established in a low-tax country primarily for investment by residents or citizens of high-tax countries. Most off-shore funds are open-ended investment companies, their assets consisting exclusively of securities, property, or cash.

An off-shore base makes investment more flexible by freeing managers from restrictions habitually imposed by the governments of their own countries as well as having access to more markets and thus added risk diversification. For example, an off-shore fund might be able to hold more than 5% of its assets in one company, something prohibited both by the Securities and Exchange Commission in the United States and the Department of Trade and Industry in the United Kingdom. It may also be empowered to invest fairly widely in unquoted securities or to establish a fund that incorporates gearing or leverage by dealing in the futures markets or in hedging operations. If the investor's home country levies taxes on capital gains realized on the sale of shares (e.g., the United States, France, Germany, and the United Kingdom), then the investment should be disposed of not by the investor himself, but by an intermediary company located in a third country, which does not levy taxes on any income or gain (tax haven), or in which the tax law contains participation exemption rules (e.g., the Netherlands) applicable to capital gains. Naturally, the absence of capital gains taxes off-shore will mean that investment switches will not incur capital gains tax. Cross-border mutual funds may be registered off-shore to minimize taxation and boost returns. In many cases, ultimately some tax will be paid in the home country, but off-shore strategies can help to minimize the tax burden or permit repatriation at the most beneficial time.

As is shown throughout this book, the importance and uses of international tax havens is widespread in its forms and structures. From shipping companies to international tennis stars, from the emigrant to the largest multinationals in the United States to captive insurance and real estate companies and film producers—the world of tax havens offers international tax benefits to the widest possible spectrum of individuals and companies, with the underlying financial structure often just as varying from one case to another.

The growing international use of tax havens is clearly illustrated throughout the text and appendixes. For example, assets in the Cayman Islands banks have risen to over $230 billion (1990) from only $85 billion in 1980. The number of foreign shares listed on the Hong Kong exchange have risen from 7 in 1986 to 67 in 1989—an annual compounded growth of 112%. Deposit banks' foreign assets in Luxembourg have risen from $103.25bn in 1983 to $251.07bn in early 1990. New company registrations in Jersey grew from 12,513 in 1978 to 28,396 in 1990. Eight of the top ten captive insurance centers are tax havens and of the top ten world's leading international banking centers, five can rightfully claim tax haven status. Hong Kong's share of the international banking market has more than doubled in the last seven years to 6%. International usage of tax havens knows no boundaries. French investors are popular users of Luxembourg investment funds (SICAVs). To the extent that the SICAV capitalizes income and capital gains, no French tax on dividends is payable until the resale of the shares.

Tax havens have acted as a catalyst for much of world trade and at present at least 50% of all the world's money is to be found in tax havens or is transferred through them. If it were not for tax havens many multinationals would be unable to profitably export their products into Europe, and in-fact many of these products would have to sell at far higher prices. Thus, despite not being financially viable the consumer would also be adversely affected—by higher prices or unavailability of the product.

Representative Tax Havens

6

The Cayman Islands

Conveniently located in the western Caribbean Sea, close by U.S. business operations, the Cayman Islands has developed into a massive financial center with a thriving banking center, no direct taxes on companies, the free and active circulation of U.S. dollars, and liberal exempt trust laws. Moreover, the Islands are an important conduit for Eurobond issues. At present the Islands are home to more than 500 international banks, more than 18,000 companies, and approximately 360 captive insurance units. Although many of these entities are shells, consisting of little more than a nameplate and a set of books, they have made the Cayman Islands one of the world's leading off-shore financial centers.

The Cayman Islands have benefited from problems experienced by other Caribbean basin centers. Drug-related scandals and sharp increases in Bahamian bank license fees, the United States' cancellation of its tax treaty with the Netherlands Antilles, and political turmoil in Panama have made the politically stable Cayman Islands an attractive Western Hemisphere haven. In effect, the policies and misfortunes of its neighbors have strengthened the position of the Islands.

The history of the Cayman Islands allowed them to write their own laws to their advantage. They took the opportunity to produce modern company and trust legislation tailormade for international purposes. Unlike the position in so many tax havens, the bulk of the Cayman population feel that they benefit from the absence of taxes.

At present there are no taxes on income, profits, capital gains, or dividend distributions, and no estate, legacy, gift, or succession duties. It is possible to form exempted companies or exempted trusts that are guaranteed by the government to be free from tax for a period generally of 15 to 50 years.

The Islands are becoming a popular base for off-shore banks. These can be:

- Unrestricted, able to operate both within the island and abroad;
- Unrestricted off-shore, able to operate anywhere outside the islands; or
- Restricted off-shore, with operations limited to transactions with named clients.

In addition to their other attributes, the Cayman Islands are particularly attractive to bankers. The Islands do not regulate the circulation of currencies, allowing funds to be brought in and out without restriction, and they boast the strictest confidentiality laws in the world, which make it a criminal offense to disclose confidential information to unauthorized persons.

It is notable that, by the end of 1988, 24 of the 25 largest banks in the world had subsidiaries or branches in the Cayman Islands. At the end of 1987, banks in the Cayman Islands reported total foreign deposits of $250 billion, almost double the level in 1982, and total external liabilities of $243 billion. According to IMF statistics, the Caymans are ranked the world's sixth-largest international banking center in terms of foreign liabilities and the seventh-largest in terms of foreign assets.

The driving force behind attracting so many of the world's major banks is the growing need among bankers to exploit every tax and technical opportunity available to maintain or boost profitability in a highly competitive industry. For this reason many banks use a Cayman Islands branch to supplement the operations of their New York branch and international banking facility. By booking certain business in the Cayman Islands, they gain exemption from taxes, which allows them to accumulate tax-free income and to time the repatriation of profits for maximum benefit rather than to avoid taxation altogether. In addition, banks are free from reserve requirements and other regulatory restraints, which reduces their overall cost of funds. These results can be achieved without any physical presence or costly overheads in the Cayman Islands. At present only 71 out of 516 banks maintain an operations presence in the Islands; the remainder are managed by others for a fee.

Swiss banks channel many fiduciary deposits through the Islands. For example, one bank takes funds and passes them to another bank for investment, collecting a fee in the process. The client retains the risk and the deposit shows up on only the second bank's balance sheet.

As a private banking center, the Islands have one of the best and most flexible trust laws available, which supplements traditional English legal principles. The normal form of trust imposes no restrictions on the settler, nor does it require that the trust document even be signed in the Cayman Islands. The rule of perpetuities applies, however, and for those anxious to establish a lengthy accumulation period, recourse should be had to the "exempt trust," a form peculiar to the Cayman Islands. All beneficiaries of an exempt trust must be resident and domiciled outside the Cayman Islands. Once this requirement is fulfilled, then a guarantee of a 50-year tax exemption may be obtained.

In addition to the standard form of exempt trust, there are two variations that are available in certain circumstances. A Section 77 exempt trust is one in which application for exempt status and tax exemption was made before the trust was established. In this case the perpetuity period can be up to 100 years. A Section 79 exempt trust is one in which some discretionary power is reserved to the trustees in the application of capital or income for all or some of the beneficiaries. Beneficiaries have no right to enforce the trust or to receive information about it. This type of trust is of value where beneficiaries may be taxable in their home jurisdictions if they have any legal rights under a trust or might be deemed the legal owners of the property or income concerned. However, because of the "Cuba Clause" contained in foreign trusts, under which the *situs* of the trust is automatically moved to another jurisdiction in the event that taxes are imposed, a Section 77 trust may not necessarily be worthwhile.

The deed of an exempt trust is filed with the Registrar, but can be inspected only by persons authorized to do so under the trust or by Cayman law. Beneficiaries cannot inspect the exempt trust deed or enforce the exempt trust, and they have no right to information about it. Keeping beneficiaries in the dark is for their own good. It is particularly important to those who are liable for tax in their own jurisdictions.

In order to set up a Cayman exempt trust (cost of CI$1,200), the Registrar must be convinced that present or likely beneficiaries are not, nor will ever become, resident or domiciled in the Islands. As such, the trust is often the key element of an arrangement seeking to sever or to prevent the formation of a connection with a high-tax jurisdiction.

Most Cayman trust services relate to *inter vivos* trusts, which are formed by an individual during his lifetime to:

- Protect his assets from the possibility of future legislation in his country of residence that might otherwise result in sequestration or forced repatriation;

- Arrange for the orderly devolution of his assets in the manner of his choice, where there exist legal restrictions in his home country on the disposition of assets by will. In particular, a person may not wish his assets located outside of his home country to be repatriated on his death. With an effective off-shore trust, that person could enjoy these assets during his lifetime and provide for them to pass to beneficiaries of his choice after his death;

- Reduce current taxation or future heavy death duties while still providing for this part of his estate to pass to his heirs or any other beneficiaries;

- Provide a foreign fund for use in personal or family emergencies; and

- Take advantage of international investment opportunities with professional management while avoiding taxation, testamentary restrictions, and other problems that would arise if he directly owned investments in other countries.

It is generally accepted among international personal financial planners that a Cayman trust or company is a very viable alternative to a Channel Island trust.

MAJOR ADVANTAGES

- The complete absence of direct taxation. There are no corporation, capital gains, payroll, property, or withholding taxes. This can be backed by a 30-year guarantee.

- The ability to accumulate profits free of tax and, for branches of subsidiaries of parent companies elsewhere, the ability to repatriate profits at most advantageous times.

- The absence of exchange control, allowing the movement of capital in and out of the colony and the opening and maintenance of accounts in any leading currency. There is also ready access to an established financial center with lines of communication with Eurocurrency.

- No restrictions on the foreign ownership of real estate and an advanced land registry system, with all titles guaranteed by the government, which allows quick and efficient transactions in property.

- An efficient processing and registry system for banks, companies, trusts, and insurance companies.

- Anonymity. Exempt companies may issue bearer shares and ordinary companies may issue shares to nominee shareholders. Exempt trust documents and banking transactions are also protected from disclosure.

■ An exempted company may receive a guarantee of 30 years against all direct taxes in the Islands. Such a company need not keep a register of members, nor file annual returns, nor hold an annual general meeting.

■ The ability to form a company with only one shareholder as well as minimum capitalization requirements.

■ A politically stable British Colony with a sophisticated local government (Diamond & Diamond).

BANKS AND TRUST COMPANIES

Cayman Islands banks and trust companies are licensed into two main categories. Class A licenses allow banking and trust operations both inside and outside the Cayman Islands. Class A companies usually deal in gold and foreign exchange. Class B licenses are limited to offshore operations, as they are excluded from trading with the Islands. Class A licensees maintain fully staffed offices, while Class B licensees tend to operate through agents.

Within the Class B category there exists a special case—the "restricted" license, which limits the holder to dealing with a clientele short list agreed upon with the regulatory authority. The restricted Class B license is suitable only for an in-house operation, such as a captive bank. The normal Class B license is thus referred to as an unrestricted license. Class B licensees are predominantly branch or subsidiary operations of international banks.

Figure 6.1 illustrates the distribution of Class A and Class B licenses as of June 30, 1988, and subdivides each class by type of operation and number of licenses issued.

The importance of Cayman Islands banks and trust companies is apparent in the statistics. On October 10, 1987, the London *Times* reported that the assets of Cayman banks and trust companies exceeded $200 billion. More recently, the *Cayman Islands Yearbook and Business Directory* (1990) reported that this figure had risen to more than $250 billion. The assets held by Cayman Class A banks and trust companies through 1988 is illustrated in Figure 6.2, which expresses both net foreign assets and total assets held.

Figure 6.1. Banking and Trust Licenses as of January 1988.

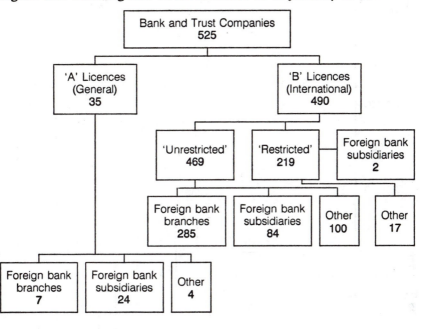

Furthermore, the Cayman Islands have become an effective conduit for Eurobond issues. They have a much more specialized role than the Netherlands Antilles, but have clearly met a need by making possible the use of a tailormade Cayman vehicle which can be formed in 24 hours. Thus, bond issuers are able to reduce their tax liabilities and other costs. With respect to Eurodollar transactions being sourced through the Cayman Islands, approximately 7% of the entire market is represented.

The authorities can now afford to refuse banking licenses to those who cannot prove that they are clean, and they emphasize that their supervisory role over banking operations starts when application is first made. Furthermore, bank references for all depositers are needed and fresh accounts of more than $10,000 (the exportable allowance in hard currency from the United States) are questioned, while bankers all do their own screening privately. A mutual assistance treaty was signed with the United States to crack down on illegitimate, criminal, and fraudulent activities in the Caymans.

Figure 6.2. Assets of Cayman Islands Class A Banks and Trust Companies.

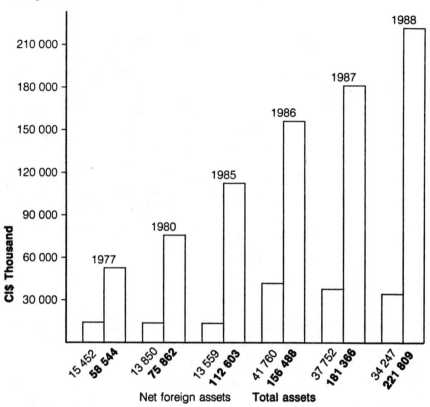

Source: Inspector of Banks and Trust Companies, Cayman Islands government

To combat the attractions of using the Cayman Islands and the Bahamas as "off-shore" banking centers, the United States set up its own "off-shore" banking market in December 1981, in the form of International Banking Facilities (IBFs). IBFs are a set of books kept within certain U.S. banks, recording all international transactions and exempting them from regulation and taxation. The main aim was to repatriate Euromarket and off-shore business to the United States, allowing U.S. banks to offer more competitive loan and deposit rates internationally and to benefit from increased efficiency, lower costs, and reduced foreign exposure by effectively carrying in off-shore business at home. At the end of 1979, foreign branches of U.S. banks reported total claims and liabilities of $364 billion, of which London branches accounted for $131 billion (36%) and the Bahamas and the Cayman Islands for $109 billion (30%). At the end of June 1987, London accounted for $147 billion (31%) and the Bahamas and the Cayman Islands for $142 billion (30%). In recent years the latter total has sometimes exceeded that of London. Thus, the impact of the IBFs has been limited, as they have been unable to duplicate all the advantages of the Cayman Islands and the Bahamas.

At present there are 525 banks on the Cayman Islands register representing 56 countries, with the largest (31%) coming from the United States, followed by Switzerland (7%) and Denmark (6%). This figure has grown since 1975, when there were 194 banks and trust companies, and 1980, when there were 324 banks and trust companies.

The growth in licensing is depicted in Figure 6.3.

The geographic distribution of Cayman Islands bank and trust company licenses has been widening progressively. As of 1990, entities representing some 56 different countries held Cayman Islands licenses. In recent years, there has been a steady decline in the number of licensees from North America, while European numbers held steady and Latin American licenses increased marginally. U.S. banks declined in numerical terms, but still hold the largest proportional share, with Swiss interests second. The geographical distribution of Cayman Islands licenses is illustrated in Table 6.1.

CAYMAN COMPANIES

Two types of companies are recognized in the Cayman Islands: "ordinary companies" and "exempted companies." An exempted company may not trade within the Cayman Islands. Some of the exemptions and privileges enjoyed by such companies are the following:

- ■ No register of members need be maintained and no annual return of members need be filed;
- ■ Bearer shares may be issued;

Figure 6.3. Cayman Islands Bank and Trust Company Licenses Recorded.

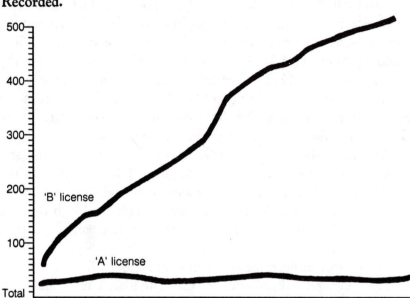

Source: Inspector of Banks and Trust Companies, Cayman Islands government

Table 6.1. Geographical Distribution of Cayman Islands Bank and Trust Company Licenses.

Region	1986	1987	1988
North America	36%	34%	32%
Western Europe	33	33	33
Latin America	12	13	13
Far East	5	5½	6
Middle East	4½	4½	5
Australasia	3	3	4
Other	6½	7	7
	100	100	100

- No annual general meeting is required;
- A guarantee against the imposition of future tax (usually for 20 years) may be obtained; and
- No official financial statements required.

These considerable benefits will best be exploited by utilizing a selling company. The ability to issue bearer shares is attractive to companies that intend to establish an overseas structure, since it provides a means of retaining the confidentiality of ultimate ownership. In addition, several good commercial reasons can be advanced to justify the existence of a selling company in the Cayman Islands that would operate as a middleman company selling goods throughout the world and accumulating profits in a tax-free zone without many questions about the origin of the goods. These reasons include:

- Geographical proximity to U.S. markets;
- Freedom from duties on goods warehoused but not distributed within the tax haven;
- Adequate communication facilities; and
- Efficient systems of warehousing goods.

There is no stamp duty on the transfer of shares and their par value may be expressed, with exchange control permission where necessary, in any currency. However, with respect to trusts, both ordinary and exempt trusts are subject to stamp duty on the trust deed. It should be remembered that, in order to make a Cayman Islands company an entity acceptable to other tax authorities, it is essential to show that actual control and management of the company emanates from the Islands and that transactions are effected at arm's length.

Many exempted companies have been incorporated in the Cayman Islands to function as investment holding companies, whereby they may hold quoted or unquoted investments throughout the world. Many trading companies also exhibit which serve to invoice goods from one country to another, acting as brokers or buying and selling in their own names on behalf of foreign suppliers located in all areas of the world. In view of the complex tax exemption and tax-free accumulation of income for transfer to capital, most of the mutual funds established in the Cayman Islands have been formed as trusts rather than as companies. This is also because the Companies Law does not allow the redemption of ordinary shares. In these instances, a mutual fund management company serves as the settler and a Cayman Islands bank specializing in trust facilities acts as the trustee. The mutual funds' management and distribution operations generally are handled by Cayman Islands exempted companies.

A summary of total company registrations by type and number and of new company registrations appears in Tables 6.2 and 6.3, respectively, at the end of the next section.

NONRESIDENT COMPANIES

Ordinary and exempted companies in the Cayman Islands may have either resident or nonresident status. Resident companies are those

■ Whose shareholders are resident in the Cayman Islands and
■ Whose business activities are conducted primarily locally within the Islands.

Resident companies may sell their shares to nonresidents without permission, since no exchange control exists.

In turn, nonresident companies are those

■ Whose shareholders are resident outside the Cayman Islands and
■ Whose business activities are conducted primarily outside the Islands.

Nonresident companies must submit the names of their shareholders to the Registrar. These companies are ordinarily entirely free from tax. They must maintain a registered office in the Cayman Islands.

Table 6.2. Total Cayman Company Registrations.

Year	Ordinary[1]	Exempt[2]	Foreign[3]	Total	Percentage increase
1975	4,129	2,320	169	6,618	11.3
1976	4,489	2,842	190	7,521	13.6
1977	4,629	3,325	204	8,158	8.5
1978	4,916	3,917	254	9,087	11.4
1979	5,372	4,888	292	10,552	16.1
1980	5,876	5,965	342	12,183	15.5
1981	6,656	7,495	386	14,537	19.3
1982	7,250	9,060	402	16,712	15.0
1983	7,304	9,797	412	17,513	4.8
1984	7,306	9,909	424	17,639	0.7
1985	7,731	10,149	467	18,347	4.0
1986	7,009	9,296	486	16,791	−8.5
1990				18,000	8.8

[1]Ordinary (1) Resident: business as usual
           (2) Nonresident: business conducted outside the Islands, except that it is necessary to maintain a registered office
[2]Exempt: tax exempted
[3]Foreign: no business conducted, registration is required
Source: Registrar of Companies, Cayman Islands government

Table 6.2 analyzes total company registrations by number and type for recent years. Table 6.3 analyzes new company registrations by number and type.

CAPTIVE INSURANCE

In addition to off-shore banking, the Cayman Islands have a second major tax haven vehicle: captive insurance. The Islands rank second in the world after Bermuda with 370 captives in 1990. Recent financial data (*Euromoney*; 1989) shows that captives had total assets of approximately $4 billion, shareholders' equity of $1.7 billion, and gross premiums per year of just under $2 billion.

The vast majority of the Cayman Islands' insurance business comes from the United States. However, as a result of U.S. presence

Table 6.3. New Cayman Islands Company Registrations.

Year	Ordinary	Exempt	Foreign	Total
1970	308	148	7	463
1971	368	203	14	585
1972	687	284	19	990
1973	767	545	50	1,362
1974	734	704	47	1,485
1975	819	428	14	1,261
1976	638	639	24	1,301
1977	710	840	26	1,576
1978	826	1,011	68	1,905
1979	1,020	1,457	56	2,533
1980	1,159	1,751	69	2,979
1981	1,151	1,836	65	3,052
1982	948	1,927	55	2,930
1983	693	1,549	42	2,284
1984	679	1,251	34	1,964
1985	745	1,226	46	2,017
1986	739	1,280	46	2,065

Source: Registrar of Companies, Cayman Islands government

in many European companies, increasing interest from Europe is currently apparent. For example, ICI PLC in Britain has a Cayman Islands' captive.

The Islands' strength as an insurance center lies partly in their longevity—they were the first of the Caribbean islands to introduce flexible off-shore insurance legislation in 1979—and particularly in their infrastructure, including banks, law firms, accountants, and insurance managers. Furthermore, the Cayman Islands do not limit the volume of business that captives can write by the amount of their capital and surplus, they do not limit their risk exposure (after reinsurance), and they have no solvency requirements. In short, the Islands give captives and managers greater flexibility to respond to changing circumstances.

One example of the type of captive that benefits from this regulating environment is a not-for-profit hospital seeking to insure itselt and its doctors against malpractice liabilities. Such an organization has no interest in accumulating excess assets off-shore and can form a break-even captive in the Cayman Islands, possibly without retaining earnings there, while satisfying local law and its own risk requirements.

It should not be overlooked that the off-shore insurance industry in the Cayman Islands owes its origins to the fact that for many years the largest multinationals had found that the conventional insurance market did not provide the flexibility of coverage or premium terms they required. Therefore, some formed their own controlled subsidiary insurance companies to insure their own risks, which were then largely reinsured internationally with terms tailormade to their own needs and claims experience.

ADVANTAGES FOR COMPANIES

Since tax-exempt incorporation with minimum regulation and maximum confidentiality are vital ingredients for any off-shore center, it is not surprising that a large number of companies have been formed in the Cayman Islands. At the end of 1988 there were more than 18,200 exempted companies registered in the Islands. Specifically they are used for

- Investment holding companies,
- Trading companies and intermediaries, and
- Brokers and buying and selling agents, trading worldwide.

New registrations seemed to peak in recent years, largely as a result of other low-cost centers, but they rebounded in 1989, possibly due to the problems in Panama. In addition, recently their corporate law was amended to allow companies to buy back their own shares. This change was designed to enable mutual funds to operate more smoothly from the territory. To date, most funds administered in the Islands have been closed-end and privately placed.

Specific Advantages

Shipping Companies.   The Cayman Islands have not succeeded in their goal of establishing a thriving foreign ship registry, because ships registered in the Islands fly the British flag and are subject to standards for British vessels. At the end of 1987, the Cayman Islands merchant shipping register carried only 702 vessels; by January 1989, the total had fallen to 601. However, a Cayman Islands corporation that owns operating ships does enjoy the following advantages:

■ The company's profits are tax-free;

■ Tonnage taxes have recently been greatly reduced and are now lower than in Greece; and

■ No need for the ship to be physically based in the Cayman Islands.

The Cayman Islands hope to compete mainly by offering ease of registration and low fees. The absence of any taxes or exchange controls makes the Islands an ideal location from which to own and operate vessels. By contrast, in the registry ports such as Isle of Man and Hong Kong, there are corporation taxes on management operations and local income tax. From a United States perspective, the Internal Revenue Service has issued a ruling that non-U.S. resident aliens or non-U.S. resident foreign corporations owning Cayman Islands registered vessels will be excluded from any tax on gross income arising from the operation of those vessels in U.S. waters.

Finance Companies.   There are no banking or exchange controls in the Cayman Islands, and funds may be freely transferred or distributed worldwide in any convertible currency. Since more than 500 banks and trust companies are licensed to do business in the Cayman Islands, this facilitates the use of and financing of an Islands finance company structure. No withholding taxes or other taxes on income or capital exist, and such funds may be remitted and repatriated free of any tax.

An exempt company or trust may be used as a finance company. Where this structure is used purely as a financial intermediary carrying on no business at all within the Cayman Islands, an exempt company or trust is the preferred entity.

In certain circumstances factoring can also be a useful extension of channelling surplus funds. Further, Cayman Islands companies are also used as bond-issuing vehicles to raise funds in the international capital markets, free of withholding or other taxes, and to channel these funds to parent companies or other companies in the same group.

Trading Companies.   There are no special regulations or taxes for trading companies. The establishment of an exempt nonresident company which simply invoices and manages off-shore operations is very popular in the Cayman Islands.

Banks and mutual fund management companies are set up to incorporate, administer, document, and invoice such activities on behalf of clients.

Trading companies range from those that simply buy goods from one country for resale to another to those that act as a central buying vehicle for a basic commodity used by a group with manufacturing plants in different locations. In either case, the profit would be earned in a tax-free location.

Licensing Companies.   The Cayman Islands licensing company is very popular among U.S. residents, especially with regard to industrial or intellectual property.

Where a jurisdiction has "controlled foreign corporation" legislation, consideration should be given to the use of an exempt trust. In a typical arrangement, the patent or other property rights are assigned to the Cayman Islands exempt trust, which then licenses other companies in the other jurisdiction to use such rights. The income of the trust can be accumulated in the Islands free of any tax.

Finally, in financing the Cayman entity, cognisance should be taken of the following benefits:

■ There are no restrictions imposed on the repatriation of funds, whether income or capital.

■ No withholding taxes are payable in the Cayman Islands.

- There are no restrictions on the payment of dividends from Cayman Islands.
- There is no exchange control.
- Profits may be accumulated free of tax.
- No treaties have been concluded with other countries (thus the Caymans enjoy secrecy).

S. Clark Thomas, an authority on tax havens, ranks the Caymans fourth out of 17 contenders for general usage, third out of nine for bearer shares, second out of seven for holding companies, the highest among no-tax havens, and third out of 14 for trusts. These are all higher rankings than those awarded to Bermuda or the Channel Islands. For the emigrant and exporter to the United States, the Cayman Islands presents a favorable jurisdiction. However, it all depends on the client's needs, where he is destined, his asset composition and other factors. In short, there are horses for courses.

Real Estate Companies.   In the 1988 calendar year, 548 developments with a total value of CI$131 million received approval. These included 333 residential projects (CI$32m), 66 commercial projects (CI$14m), 74 condominium projects (CI$42m), and four hotels (CI$28m).

The Cayman Islands's limited land area, combined with growing tourist and financial incentives, results in a medium with a healthy turn-over at increasing prices.

Even though there are no property taxes, the annual revenue from this industry has surpassed that from company registration and from bank and trust company license fees. This revenue accounts for in excess of 10% of total government revenue.

The growing tourism industry, bolstered by the proximity to North America and the tranquility of the Islands, continues to demand development. More than 80% of the land area remains undeveloped, and the ownership of property is a prerequisite for obtaining residency.

There are a number of sites with good potential. As the properties become more subdivided, these will decrease, thereby causing price increases.

There is only one golf course, and it serves mainly
the Hyatt Hotel. There is no doubt that another is sorely
the lands are readily available in the eastern part of the

INCENTIVES TO LOCAL INDUSTRIES

The Cayman Islands government has introduced incentives to encourage the establishment of local industries. The most important
concession is that customs duty may be waived in full or in part in
accordance with the following guidelines:

- Industries catering for the export market with an investment
  exceeding CI$50,000 and employing at least four Cayman
  Islanders for a minimum of five years may be granted full
  waiver of customs import duty on building materials and
  equipment, machinery, and tools of trade. Materials for use
  in the manufacturing process may also be granted a waiver of
  import duty.

- Industries providing for the local market with an investment
  exceeding CI$25,000 and employing at least four Cayman
  Islanders for a minimum of three years may be granted a
  waiver of customs import duty on building materials and
  equipment, machinery, and tools of trade.

- A company not requiring a license to operate under the local
  companies (control) law, investing a sum of at least
  CI$10,000 in a new industry and employing at least two
  Cayman Islanders, may be entitled to import duty conces-
  sions, depending on the nature of the application (Cayman
  Islands Executive Council.)

TAX CONSIDERATIONS FOR THE U.S. INVESTOR

From the point of view of the U.S. investor, all of the benefits of the
Cayman Islands tax haven hold true. The Islands are conveniently
located to U.S. interests. There is no direct taxation. Properly organized companies and trusts may qualify for additional tax exemptions.

The large number of banks licensed in the Islands offer highly sophisticated international banking services. Cayman Islands law provides for the free circulation of currencies and a high degree of confidentiality in banking and business transactions.

However, certain provisions of the Internal Revenue Code must be considered before a U.S. investor decides to take advantage of the Islands system.

The Passive Foreign Investment Company

The passive foreign investment company (PFIC) can be applied to any U.S. person who owns stock in any corporation. The U.S. stockholder of a PFIC is assessed an interest charge as well as a deferral tax amount in relation to earnings of the PFIC.

Although the PFIC rules were aimed primarily at passive foreign investments, many U.S. owned foreign companies that conduct active businesses may come under its definition. A PFIC is defined as any foreign corporation with 75% or more of its gross income for the taxable year consisting of passive income or with 50% or more of the average yearly value of its assets consisting of assets that produce, or are held for the production of, passive income. Passive income includes dividends, interest, passive rents and royalties, annuities, profits from the sale of property that gives rise to the above income or to no income, foreign currency gains, and interest income. There are exceptions and special rules for certain foreign corporations. Passive income for purposes of the PFIC definition does not include any income derived in the active conduct of a banking insurance business by an institution licensed to do business as a bank in the United States. Many of the corporations established in the Cayman Islands by U.S. individuals or entities which hold assests such as cash, stocks, or real estate are classified as PFICs. When the foreign corporation makes a distribution to the U.S. shareholders or when the U.S. shareholder disposes of the stock, the U.S. person is then subject to a deferred tax and interest charge on the profit from the sale of the PFIC stock or the receipt of an excess distribution from the PFIC. The tax is determined by using the current top statutory rules.

A U.S. shareholder is able to avoid the scenarios described previously by electing to treat the PFIC as a qualified electing fund (QEF). The election is effective for the shareholder's taxable year for which it is made and all subsequent taxable years. A shareholder of a QEF must include in its gross income annually its pro rata share of the PFIC's current earnings and profits. The adverse tax consequences of owning stock in a PFIC may be reduced considerably with proper planning.

Real Estate Purchases

When U.S. investors produce Cayman real estate a major decision is made whether to hold title as an individual or within a Cayman Islands company. This decision will be based on whether the real estate will be used as a residence, a vacation home, a rental property, or land held for speculative purposes.

If the real estate is to be used as a residence or a vacation home, it would be best to hold title as an individual. By doing this, the entire interest expense may be claimed on the owner tax return as either the primary residence or as a second home. U.S. taxpayers are also allowed special treatment for gain on the sale of a principal residence.

If a property is purchased to be held as a long-term rental, it would also be best to hold title as an individual. That way, it will be possible for rental losses to be taken on the owner's individual tax return.

Under this particular situation, if the rental property had been purchased and held within a Cayman Islands corporation, the losses could not be taken on the owner's tax return, and the rental income reduced by deductions would be classified as foreign personal holding company income (FPHCI). If the income is described in this manner, it may subject the company to classification as a passive foreign investment company (PFIC). The tax provisions relating to the PFIC can be hazardous as is discussed above. If the foreign corporation is engaged in an active rental trade or business, the rents received from unrelated persons will not be classified as FPHCI, but an active trade or business requires a certain level of participation. In order to deter-mine if the corporation would be considered to be in the active con-duct of a rental trade or business, it is necessary to review the facts and circumstances of each case (Cayman Islands Yearbook 1990.)

Land or real estate held for speculative purposes should be owned by the individual, not a Cayman Islands corporation. Again, if the land is held by a Cayman Islands corporation, the corporation may be classified as a PFIC.

Cayman Islands Corporation

If a Cayman Islands corporation is engaged in an active trade or busi-ness in the Cayman Islands, it is possible that the U.S. shareholders will not be taxed currently on the corporation's earnings. Assuming the corporation is not engaged in a U.S. trade or business, there should also be a corporate-level tax. The U.S. shareholders will be taxed when they receive distributions or dividends. As a result of be-ing an active business the company is not labeled as a PFIC and the U.S. corporation is able to accumulate profits tax free.

7

Liechtenstein

The principality of Liechtenstein offers the benefits of a Swiss level of financial stability and professional services with virtual freedom from taxation. There is a double-taxation agreement with Austria, but, this apart, Liechtenstein can be classified as a zero-tax haven which does not enjoy a reduced rate of withholding taxes on income flowing in from other countries.

Liechtenstein's attractions as a tax haven are based on its favorable tax structures, its flexible and unique attitude toward company and trust formation, political stability, a central European location, excellent telecommunications, good professional and banking services, and bank secrecy laws.

An important feature of the law is the wide range of available forms of organization. As elsewhere in Europe, it is possible to set up limited companies and limited and unlimited partnerships. Liechtenstein is the only jurisdiction in Europe with a body of law and practice governing trusts of the type familiar in the English-speaking world. There are also two forms of organization having some of the characteristics of both companies and trusts. These are the *Anstalt* (or establishment) and the *Stiftung* (or foundation). Many tax haven intermediaries follow one of these two forms. A valuable peculiarity of both *Stiftung* and *Anstalt* organizations is that they can behave as if they were bodies corporate with limited liability when acting as investors or in the conduct of a trade or business. However, when they distribute income or assets, they can do so in accordance with the more subtle and flexible rights that can be conferred by the equivalent of a trust deed. One important distinction between them is that an *Anstalt* is treated under English traditional law, while a *Stiftung* is not. Contrary to English law, under which trusts generally operate, Liechtenstein law prohibits neither an accumulation of proceeds nor perpetuity. Thus, a trust is far more flexible and can be created for an unspecified period.

Including the forms already mentioned, the organizations commonly used for Liechtenstein tax havens are:

- *Treuhanderschaf* (trust);
- *Aktiengesellschaft* (company limited by shares);
- *Stiftung* (foundation);
- *Anstalt* (establishment);
- *Verein* (association);
- *Kommanditaktiengesellschaft* (limited partnership with a share capital);
- *Kollektivgesellschaft* (partnership);
- *Einfache Gesellschaft* (simple partnership);
- *Kommanditgesellschaft* (limited partnership);
- *Treuunternehmen* (business trust); and
- *Genossenschaft* (registered cooperative society).

The most widely used of these are discussed in more detail in the sections that follow. Table 7.1 compares the tax treatment and legal requirements for each. Table 7.2 compares fees and annual costs for each.

Liechtenstein has no import exchange controls. As it has no fiduciary system of its own, it is dependent upon taxes, duties, and loans for its income. Like Switzerland, Liechtenstein is a member of the European Free Trade Association (EFTA) and consequently benefits from the absence of tariff duties and the various tax harmoniza-

Table 7.1. Liechtenstein Companies and Trusts: Tax Treatment and Legal Requirements.

	Corporation[1] (Aktiengesellschaft)	Establishment[2] (Anstalt)	Foundation (Stiftung)		Business trust (Treuunternehmen)	Trust (Treuhänderschaft)
			With commercial activities	Other		
Tax treatment						
1. Minimum capital	SwF50,000	30,000	30,000	30,000	30,000	Nil
2. Stamp tax on capital: Upon formation	3.0%	3.0%[3]	3.0%[3]	0.2%[4]	3.0%[3]	Nil
3. Income tax	Nil	Nil	Nil	Nil	Nil	Nil
4. Capital tax on net assets (Minimum, SwF1,000)	0.1%	0.1%	0.1%[5]	0.1%[5]	0.1%	0.1%
5. Coupon tax on dividends and other monetary benefits	4.0%	Nil	Nil	Nil	Nil[6]	Nil[6]
Legal requirements						
1. Disclosure by: Registration of statutes/deeds or Depositing of statutes/deeds	Yes	Yes	Yes	Either registration or deposition[7]	Yes	Either registration or deposition[7]
2. Financial statements: To be filed with Tax authorities	Yes	Yes, if with commercial activities[8]	Yes	No[9]	Yes, if with commercial activities[8]	No
3. Auditors: Compulsory	Yes	Yes, if with commercial activities	Yes	No	Yes, if with commercial activities	No

[1] Holding corporations whose share capital is at least SwF500,000 are subject to the stamp tax on security transactions.

[2] Establishments whose capital is divided into shares are treated as corporations in all respects.

[3] Upon request, the rate may be reduced for capital of SwF5 million or more to 1.5%, for capital of SwF10 million or more to 1%.

[4] Minimum, SwF200.

[5] Capital tax is reduced to 0.075% on net assets in excess of SwF2 million and to 0.05% on excess of SwF10 million.

[6] Coupon tax of 4% is payable if beneficial interest is derived from a security document.

[7] Registration or deposition of statutes or deeds is compulsory, but choice is optional.

[8] If not involved in commercial activities and the articles do not provide for such activities, a declaration to this effect may be submitted to the registry in lieu of filing audited annual accounts to the tax authorities.

[9] If registered with the commercial register, a declaration must be filed annually as described under note 8 above.

Table 7.2. Liechtenstein Companies and Trusts: Fees and Annual Costs.

	Corporation (Aktiengesellschaft)	Establishment (Anstalt)[1] Business trust (Treuunter-nehmen)	Foundation (Stiftung)	Trust (Treuhandschaft)
Incorporation fees				
Stamp tax (minimum)	SwF1,500	900	200	Nil
Fee for commercial register (minimum)	500	500	500	250
Lawyer's formation fee (approx)	2,500	2,500	2,500	2,500
Other expenses (approx)	300	300	300	300
Total	SwF4,800	4,200	3,500	3,050
Annual costs				
Capital tax (minimum)	SwF1,000	1,000	1,000	Nil
Fees for directorship, trustee, etc (approx)	2,500	2,500	2,500	2,500
Fees for legal representation (approx)	500	500	500	500
Fees for auditors (pro memoria)	?	?	?	?
Fees for other local services (pro memoria)	?	?	?	?
4% coupon tax on distributions (pro memoria)	?[2]	—[2]	—	—[2]

[1]Establishments whose capital is divided into shares are treated as corporations in all respects.
[2]Coupon tax is payable by business trusts and other trusts, if beneficial interest is derived from a security document.

The above is a general guideline and subject to changes in particular cases.

tion objectives of the other original six members and three additional members of the EFTA.

Like Switzerland, there are no restrictions on transfer of dividends, royalties, interest, and other earnings. Repatriation of both debt and equity capital may be remitted freely, without any limitations. The authorities will guarantee free convertibility of exchange, but Liechtenstein does not have a bilateral treaty providing investment guarantees against inconvertibility of currency.

Liechtenstein does not have a free trade zone *per se*. However, under the Customs Treaty of 1923 with Switzerland, goods from the two countries may circulate freely, with the exception of a few restrictions in traffic between one canton and another.

Liechtenstein permits the invoicing of foreign trade documents in any freely convertible currency and in the currency of the importing country. Importers are not required to make prior deposits in local funds, while export proceeds are not required to be surrendered to the banks.

Liechtenstein has one tax treaty—with Austria—to avoid double taxation. Under the agreement Liechtenstein exempts interest from withholding tax and does not tax income from shipping and aircraft income earned by Austrian companies from operations in Liechtenstein. In the absence of an information exchange service or of judicial assistance in fiscal matters related to Switzerland's numerous treaties, Liechtenstein offers greater banking secrecy than Switzerland.

FAVORED-TREATMENT COMPANIES: HOLDING COMPANIES AND DOMICILIARIES

Liechtenstein gives particularly favorable tax treatment to companies that choose Liechtenstein as their residence without doing any business there. An extra inducement to set up a base in Liechtenstein is the flexibility of company-structure legislation. The two main categories of favored-treatment companies are holding companies and domiciliary companies. Holding companies are defined as companies whose main purpose is to participate in other countries. They can hold shares in other local or foreign companies, or in local or foreign property, including patents, trademarks, licenses, and copyrights. If they hold real estate, they must pay the corporate net worth tax of 0.2%. Domiciliary companies have a corporate seat but no business activities in Liechtenstein. The most common forms are stock corporations (*Aktiengesellschaft*) and *Anstalts*.

Annual meetings of holding and domiciliary companies need not take place in Liechtenstein, and the founders need not have Liechtenstein nationality or be residents. However, these companies must appoint a local representative, either an individual or a partnership, resident in Liechtenstein and of Liechtenstein nationality, and one member of the board must be domiciled there. By the beginning of 1988, there were at least 40,000 registered companies in Liechtenstein, almost two per capita of population.

Tax legislation favorable to the economy has led to the establishment of an efficient highly technical industry, most of whose products are exported. The value of the goods exported by the members of the Chamber of Industry and Commerce has risen since 1950 from SwF15 million to more than SwF1.3 billion. Most goods are exported to the countries of the European Community. Liechenstein banks employ close to 1,000 people and show a balance sheet total of more than 10 billion SFs.

The tax liabilities of the holding and domiciliary companies are few and light. On formation, duty of 2% of the contributed capital is payable and another 2% is levied on subsequent stock issues. There are also registration fees and stamp duties. Holding and domiciliary companies pay no profits tax and pay net worth tax at the reduced rate of 0.1%, with a minimum of SwF1,000. Stock companies are subject to 4% withholding tax and interest on medium- and long-term loans. The anonymity of the actual owner of a company is guaranteed by the strongest privacy legislation in Europe, if not in the world.

The reasons advocating the founding of a Liechtenstein-based holding or domicile company are most favored when holding securities, purchasing real estate, importing and exporting commercial goods, and utilizing patents. Common tax advantages not mentioned earlier include:

■ Holding and domiciliary companies are treated alike as base companies if they are engaged in no Liechtenstein business. Both may maintain an office in Liechtenstein with one or several employees without losing their privileged tax status as long as they do not engage in commerce or industry in Liechtenstein.

■ Royalties are not taxable, while interest is subject to a 4% tax. There is an 8.4% turnover tax on goods transferred for sale and on imported goods. The rate is 5.6% for other goods. The turnover tax is paid by the consumer.

■ Estates are taxed at low rates of from 1 to 5%. However, inheritances are subject to higher taxes, ranging from 10% on the first SwF50,000 and graduating to 50% for estates over SwF750,000.

Loan-to-equity capital ratios normally may not exceed 3:1, although a 5:1 ratio may be acceptable to the authorities.

The incorporation of a holding company is particularly easy in Liechtenstein. No permit is required to establish a company, except for banks, finance and insurance companies, investment funds, trust companies, and auditing firms.

TRUST ORGANIZATIONS

Liechtenstein is known for its developed and well-defined trust law. There are three primary forms of trust organization.

"The *Treuhanderschaft* is a private or real trust, also known as a 'specific business trust,' in which the identity of the settler is kept secret by having trustees hold and administer trust assets. It is not a separate legal entity. The deed may provide for limited or unlimited personal liability of participants or third parties. The trustee has a legal claim to reimbursements of all the necessary expenses incurred by him for the trust and may receive a salary." (Diamond 1986.)

The *Treuunternehmen* is used for commercial purposes. A trust is formed with relative ease and may be created to invest capital, distribute profits, and assign beneficial shares for family welfare or charitable reasons. The trust is not a legal entity, it is, therefore, not entitled to the tax privileges of a holding or domiciliary company.

A third type of trust found only in Anglo-American and Liechtenstein legislation is the trust settlement. This is not a company with its own legal personality, but a special legal relationship; therefore it is sometimes called a "trust relationship." A trust settlement involves transfer of any asset to a trustee for administration or for specific uses as determined by the settler. It is in the trustee's own name as an independent legal entity. A major disadvantage of a trust settlement is that, in the event of an insolvency of the trustee, the settler and beneficiary must share their claims with the other creditors.

COMPANIES LIMITED BY SHARES (CORPORATIONS)

Companies limited by shares must have predetermined capital, divided into shares, factions, or quotas. Shares may be with or without par value, registered or bearer or both. The company limited by shares (*Aktiengesellschaft* or AG) can be formed by one shareholder.

Capital may be in Swiss francs or in any one of the other recognized currencies, and negotiable profit-sharing certificates may be issued. Corporations with variable capital may issue registered shares only, and the capital may be increased by issuing new shares or reduced by repayment of shares. A corporation with variable capital may later re-issue any shares repurchased, and at least 10% of the net profit must be allocated to the reserve fund until it reaches the minimum designated in the articles. The corporation must keep proper books. This is the responsibility of the Directors. However, domiciliary companies and foundations (except for domiciliary companies engaged in commercial activities), or family-owned corporations do not have to provide books to the government. By contrast, corporations are required to publish "true and complete" annual financial statements. Corporations issuing bearer shares must file financial details with the Commercial Registrar, but can preserve their anonymity by having a Liechtenstein representative register the company and by issuing bearer shares only. Companies limited by shares are subject to the normal capital and income taxes, unless they are holding or domiciliary companies, which are exempt from profits tax and receive low capital tax rates.

Aktiengesellschaft (company limited by shares)

The AG is a standard form of limited-liability company. "The following is a list of some of the beneficial uses of a Liechtenstein AG:

- The creation of an entity through which securities, real estate, and various other assets, perhaps in several jurisdictions around the world, may be held and managed;
- A means of avoiding or reducing probate formalities where assets are held in several countries;
- A potential form of protection against income and capital taxes, death and gift duties, expropriation, or confiscation;
- A means of providing confidentiality so that, for example, the name of the actual beneficial owner of the company and its assets are not disclosed to the world at large;
- A center for holding patent rights and a useful conduit for collecting royalties;
- A means of arranging management and consultancy services, franchise agreements, and commission-collecting activities together with other commercial operations; and
- To facilitate the launching of a venture in a new country or to expand an existing business across national boundaries through a conveniently placed low-tax jurisdiction." (Diamond 1986.)

ANSTALT

The *Anstalt*, or establishment, is a creation peculiar to Liechtenstein which can be adapted to be all things to all tax avoiders. It has a separate legal personality. Its capital may or may not be divided into shares. A benefit of no share capital is that the *Anstalt* is exempt from withholding tax and the founder can allocate the profits as he likes. The minimum paid-in capital must be SwF30,000 where there are no participation shares and SwF50,000 where there are.

The tax liabilities of an *Anstalt* start with 3% formation duty and contributed capital. *Anstalts* that carry on business activities in Liechtenstein pay the normal rates of profits tax and net worth tax, but *Anstalts* with no local activities pay net worth tax at a reduced rate of 0.1% (minimum SwF1,000) and are exempt from profits tax. *Anstalts* divided into shares are subject to withholding tax on dividends, so most *Anstalts* do not have any share capital.

Like corporations, *Anstalts* need a Board of Directors, which may consist of just one member provided that he is domiciled in Liechtenstein. The *Anstalt* also requires a resident legal representative. Usually the Liechtenstein adviser helping with the formation of an *Anstalt* will undertake to be both the one required domiciled member of the board and the local representative.

Anstalts are used in many ways similar to those of the holding and domiciliary AGs, for example, to hold patents, trademarks, and copyrights and to take holdings in other companies. Their advantage over the AG lies in the greater flexibility of secrecy of their operations—in fact, the CIA is known to have used them. The founder's certificate of an *Anstalt* is often transferred in blank, similar to a bearer share.

Anstalts are not required to be profit making nor are they obliged to be commercial or industrial undertakings. One of the primary functions of *Anstalts* exploited by foreign companies is to hold financial or controlling interests in overseas firms. Unlike many tax havens, where financing activities are a principal function of holding or trading company operations, Liechtenstein does not have any restrictions on the debt:equity ratio. *Anstalts* are often enlisted for the management of large fortunes for third parties. In this case, it would be expedient to make a clear separation between the *Anstalt's* assets and the assets to be managed. The *Anstalt* is in this case merely a management company for a particular fortune.

An *Anstalt* that has the sole purpose of either administering its assets or acting as a holding vehicle need not appoint auditors or file annual accounts. An *Anstalt's* liabilities are limited to the assets owned. As mentioned previously, one of the most attractive features of the *Anstalt* is that the domicile and nationality of its founder are of no relevance. An *Anstalt* may also be governed by the country laws of the founder if so desired, thus making them extremely flexible.

STIFTUNG

A second entity unique to Liechtenstein is the *Stiftung*, or foundation. It has many of the characteristics of a discretionary trust. In many ways it is like a charitable foundation, except that it has private, noncharitable beneficiaries. One New York attorney has described the *Stiftung* as the equivalent of a family Red Cross. If a family member asks the *Stiftung's* board for money, he is likely to get it; an outsider will not.

The founder of a *Stiftung* does not acquire founder's rights. The *Stiftung* is formed with an endowment of funds in the minimum amount of SwF30,000. The members of the *Stiftung's* board of administrators do not hold title to the foundation's funds in their own name. The funds must be used for the purposes set forth in the articles, but the sole purpose may be the maintenance of a particular family.

Normally, a *Stiftung* is created to make grants of revenue from foundation property. According to law, there are two types of foundations:

1. The simple family foundation for providing education or support to family members, which is used most often, and

2. The mixed family foundation where the settled property is to be partially or additionally allocated to purposes outside the family.

In both cases the settlement of property is a donation without the founder receiving any legal or economic registerable equivalent. The settler may be an individual, corporation, or partnership who gives the foundation its constitution and specifies the form of administration and benefits. *Stiftungs* may not engage in any sort of commercial business, although there is one exception, when commercial operations are required to attain the noncommercial objects of the *Stiftung*.

The settler of a *Stiftung* can remain anonymous by nominating the Liechtenstein adviser as a trustee or by giving him a power of attorney. The *Stiftung* is fully exempted from any property, income, and earnings taxes, being subject only to modest capital tax of 0.1% on net assets (net property), but at least SwF1,000 per annum. Capital tax is reduced to 0.05-0.075% provided the property is in excess of SwF2 million. A withholding tax of 4% is levied on dividend payments.

Americans utilizing the *Stiftung* or who are beneficiaries of a *Stiftung* will be unable to determine whether the U.S. tax authorities will classify the *Stiftung* as a trust or as an association taxable as a corporation for U.S. tax purposes. As such U.S. citizens should take care when establishing a *Stiftung*. With proper planning the *Stiftung* can be of tremendous benefit to U.S. citizens. Often the *Stiftung* can benefit from low taxes although being controlled by U.S. trust law.

BENEFITS TO INDIVIDUALS

Tax havens offer tremendous incentives for different high-net-worth individuals to either operate business transactions or reside in the area.

High-Income, Nonemigrant Celebrities

International sports stars, motion picture celebrities, and best-selling authors may have very substantial earnings over a relatively short working life. To these people, a Liechtenstein tax haven may offer a large measure of tax relief.

In a relatively simple case, a film star may create an *Anstalt*, which makes a contract with a film studio. The film studio will want some kind of personal guarantee from the star that the services promised by the *Anstalt* will be provided, typically, the *Anstalt* will pay the film star a small salary, which will suffer tax in his country of residence, and the star will then use the residue that accumulates in the *Anstalt* as a pension fund for his old age. Depending on the star's country of citizenship, it may be possible to pay the star a large salary which will not be taxed in his country of residence because it was earned in a third jurisdiction.

Such a scheme—in either version—is sensitive to attack on two counts. First, the country in which the film star resides may disregard the intermediary vehicle and treat its income as the income of the individual film star, and the country in which the income arises may disregard the intermediary vehicle and treat the income as that of the individual film star. The second hazard is of considerable importance when the intermediary vehicle is not a Liechtenstein *Anstalt* but a Swiss company or entity that is entitled to the benefit of a double-taxation agreement with the country in which the income arises. In that case, looking right through the intermediary would expose the income to tax for which relief would have been given under the relevant treaty.

When deciding on the different jurisdictions to operate out of, consideration should be given to the consistency of their legal structure (i.e., it is better to operate out of jurisdictions that will recognize Anglo-Saxon/U.S. type trusts) rather than taking a risk and operating in one jurisdiction that has an entirely different set of legal structures for the same purpose.

Emigrants: Making a Liechtenstein Stop-Over

Through careful planning, individuals who intend to emigrate from their own countries may escape gift taxes and death taxes of various kinds. One may leave country A a rich man and arrive in country B a (relatively) poor man, having made a variety of gifts or somehow having dropped off assets into a *Stiftung* or trust in Liechtenstein after leaving country A and before arriving in B. A Liechtenstein *Anstalt* is free from exchange controls and is often a safe haven for an emigrant's capital as well as investment income particularly interest income.

For currency purposes, the best option is for the emigrant to remain external to his new country of residence. If this is not possible, the emigrant may try to keep the bulk of his investments in, for example, a Liechtenstein *Anstalt* which is free from exchange controls.

8

Luxembourg

The Grand Duchy of Luxembourg is considered by many to be Europe's leading tax haven. Its appeal lies in a combination of advantages: a favorable tax system; stringent laws for bank secrecy and investor confidentiality; an expanding diversity in financial services, including private banking, portfolio management, and insurance; proximity to Western European financial centers; good communications facilities; a relatively light regulatory structure; a high degree of discretion lodged in governmental authorities; political stability; and the respectability that comes with membership in the European Economic Community (EEC).

Luxembourg's tax system imposes no local income or withholding taxes on investment revenues, no inheritance investment tax on the assets of nonresidents, no stamp duty on stock or bond transactions, and no value added tax on dealings in gold or gold coins.

The nation's tax system has encouraged an influx of banks, investment funds, and insurance operations. The absence of tax on investment income is highly favorable when compared with Switzerland's 35% annual rate on interest income and bank deposits. Investment companies based in Luxembourg are able to avoid tax on dividends and interest earned on Euromarkets and the double taxation of dividends subject to withholding at the source.

Luxembourg has also found a niche in the insurance industry. Since 1985 its lenient tax laws have induced 43 companies to establish captive reinsurance operations in Luxembourg. Recent arrivals include such well-known companies as Volvo, Philips, Saab, Electrolux, and Banque Nationale de Paris. Recently, New York City-based American International Group, one of the world's leading property and casualty insurance underwriters, signed a deal to begin its own Luxembourg reinsurance operation.

The absence of withholding tax on interest payments has caused the Luxembourg banking and financial community to oppose the European Commission's plan to impose a 15% tax-at-source on the savings and bank income of all European Community residents. The main loser from this proposal would have been Luxembourg, while the victor would have been Switzerland, for the proposal would have ended an important advantage. For very good reasons, the famed "Coupon Express" travels weekly from Brussels to Luxembourg so that holders of bearer Eurobonds can exchange their bond coupons for interest payments at banks in the Grand Duchy.

Table 8.1 summarizes the current rates of withholding taxes applied to the residents of the named states.

HOLDING COMPANIES

For many, the real attraction of Luxembourg is its holding companies, which benefit from both a high degree of confidentiality and a favorable tax position. To qualify as a holding company, an enterprise must meet the strict requirements imposed by Luxembourg law.

Luxembourg holding companies may issue bearer shares, which serve to conceal the identity of the shareholders. In addition, Luxembourg holding companies are not required to produce proper annual accounts. In this regard, Luxembourg holding companies are exempt from the EEC's Fourth Company Law Directive under which companies of a certain size are required to provide a minimum level of financial information.

Luxembourg holding companies are exempt from income or capital gains tax and from withholding tax on dividends paid to shareholders. Luxembourg's regular corporate income tax rates run to 40%. It must be emphasized that an enterprise that fails to meet all of the

Table 8.1. Luxembourg Withholding Taxes.

Recipient	Dividends (portfolio)[1]	Dividends (substantial holdings)[2]	Bond Interest[5]	Royalities[6]
Resident corporations and individuals	15%	—[3]	—	Nil
Non-resident corporations and individuals:				
Non-treaty	15	15%	—	12%
Treaty:				
Austria	15	5	—	—[7]
Belgium	15	10	—	—
Brazil	15	15	—	12
Denmark	15	5	—	—
Finland	15	5	—	5[8]
France	15	5	—	—
Germany	15	10	—	5
Ireland, Republic of	15	5	—	—
Italy	15	15	—	10
Morocco	15	10	—	10
Netherlands	15	2.5	—	—
Norway	15	5	—	—
Sweden	15	5	—	—
United Kingdom	15	5	—	5[9]
United States[4]	7.5	5	—	—

[1]Dividends and interest paid by Luxembourg holding companies or investment funds are exempt from withholding taxes.

[2]A substantial holding is considered to arise:

  a. Austria, Denmark, Germany, Ireland, Morocco, Norway, Sweden, the Netherlands, and the United Kingdom—Where the recipient company holds at least 25% of the Luxembourg company's shares or voting power.

  b. Belgium—Where the recipient owns a 25% investment (or an investment of LFr 250 million at cost). Such investment may be held by several Belgian companies, provided one owns at least 50% of the shares of each of the others.

  c. Finland, France—Where the recipient owns a 25% investment. Several Finnish or, respectively, French companies may together own 25% as long as one of the companies owns more than 50% in each of the others.

  d. United States—Where the recipient U.S. company has held during the entire year (alone or with up to three other U.S. companies each holding at least 10% of the shares) 50% of the Luxembourg shares and where a maximum of 25% of the gross income of the Luxembourg company originates from interest and dividends from non-group companies.

[3]Dividends paid to a holding company do not benefit from this exemption.

[4]The tax reduction applies only when the beneficiary has no permanent establishment in Luxembourg.

[5]Bond interest is not subject to withholding tax, except for interest that represents a right to profit participation. These profit-participation bonds will be subject to a withholding tax when the holder is resident in the following countries: Belgium, Brazil, the Netherlands at a rate of 15%; France, Italy, Morocco at a rate of 10%.

[6]Royalties from artistic rights have a reduced standard rate of 10%.

[7]Royalties paid to Austria are taxable at 10% if the Austrian company owns more than 50% of the Luxembourg company.

[8]Royalties from trademarks and know-how are taxable at 5%.

[9]Royalties on films are treated as business income.

requirements for a holding company will be subject to the full rate of corporate income tax and will not qualify for exemption. Luxembourg law does not permit a "mixed" holding company that is both a holding company and commercially active.

Resident companies, which are those incorporated in Luxembourg or that have their principal place of business in Luxembourg, are liable for a corporations tax of 36% on worldwide income. Clearly, a resident company is of no use to an enterprise that intends to benefit from Luxembourg law. However, no income tax will be required if the enterprise ensures that it qualifies as a holding company by holding or owning only

- Shares in a Luxembourg or foreign corporation;
- Bonds or debentures;
- Government securities;
- Cash, foreign currencies, or gold;
- Deposits with banks and financial institutions;
- Shares and other interests in real estate companies;
- Notes evidencing loans to corporations in which it holds a participation; and
- Patents, although normally not trademarks.

A Luxembourg holding company may not hold

- Interests in general or limited partnerships;
- Interests in an *Anstalt*;
- Real estate other than for its own office;
- Patent licenses, unless they complement patents already owned; or
- Commodities.

Moreover, a holding company may not act as a bank. Under some circumstances a group of multinational companies can use a

Luxembourg holding company to finance any or all of the companies within the group, even though the holding company does not hold direct share interests in all of the affiliated companies. Such a financial holding company can be used as an international finance subsidiary. It is also possible to establish a banking financial holding company.

Luxembourg law makes provision for a luxury holding company, the *milliardaire*. A *milliardaire* is a holding company that has assets of at least LFr1 billion and that has been set up by a foreign company. Like ordinary Luxembourg holding companies, the *milliardaire* holding company pays no income or capital gains tax and no withholding tax on the dividends it pays to shareholders. The *milliardaire* holding company is generally treated in the same way as a standard holding company. However, instead of the annual 0.2% subscription tax, it is liable to a tax on distribution of interest, dividends, profit-sharing bonuses, and remunerations, to a tax on capital contributions at the rate of 1% on the value of the subscribed capital at the time of incorporation or increase in capital, and certain taxes on interest paid.

It is important to note that Luxembourg holding companies are expressly excluded from the benefits of the tax treaty network. Dividend and interest income received by Luxembourg holding companies will be subject to the maximum rates of withholding tax in the source country. However, no Luxembourg withholding tax exists on dividends distributed or interest paid by a holding company. Therefore, it may be necessary to use a combination of low-tax countries to achieve the shift of profits to the tax-free Luxembourg holding company without incurring high rates of withholding tax. The restrictions imposed on Luxembourg holding companies, their comparatively high operating costs, and the lack of tax-treaty protection make the Netherlands, the Netherlands Antilles, or Switzerland preferable as the base for certain types of holding operations.

As a result of low withholding tax between the French, British and Spanish companies and the Netherlands Company as well as the participation exemption obtainable in the Netherlands, the Luxembourg holding company will be able to reduce its previous withholding taxes substantially, by interposing a Netherlands company between its three other entities in Europe.

Table 8.2. reflects the status of Luxembourg's tax treaties.

BANKING

Luxembourg's main banking business is concerned with the Eurobond and syndicated credit markets. Recently, what has emerged is a rapid growth in investment banking, with particular emphasis on portfolio management of fiduciary accounts. This used to be the Swiss banks' specialty, even though a lot of the cash deposited with them by rich foreigners was reinvested via Luxembourg. Lower costs, less exchange control measures, better secrecy, and the belief that a Luxembourg bank account may be less of a stigma in the eyes of foreign reserve officials than a Swiss account have allowed Luxembourg to capture much of the old Swiss banking markets. Further, the Grand Duchy has refused to yield to EEC pressure to levy value added tax on residents' gold transactions, making it cheaper to buy gold there than elsewhere in the EEC.

A central attraction of Luxembourg's banks is the Grand Duchy's stringent bank-secrecy laws, which offer clear advantages to those who seek privacy. These advantages have become more apparent during the time that Swiss bank secrecy has eroded. As U.S. regulators penetrate farther beyond the veil of secrecy surrounding Swiss banking, money has begun pouring out of Switzerland into the banks of the nearby Grand Duchy. Although the flow had gone largely unnoticed, foreigners' deposits in Luxembourg banks jumped nearly 40% in 1986 to an estimated $160 billion. In effect, this put the Grand Duchy on a par with Switzerland and within reach of what statistics suggest is the largest money haven in the world, the Cayman Islands, with its roughly $200 billion in deposits.

This flow of funds is demonstrated in Figure 8.1, which shows the relative amounts of foreign deposits in ten leading money havens, and in Figure 8.2, which compares foreign deposits in Luxembourg and Swiss banks at critical points in the recent history of the bank-secrecy laws of the two nations.

Table 8.2. Luxembourg Tax Treaties.

Country	Date of treaty and amendments thereto	Applicable since
Austria	October 18, 1962	January 1, 1961
Belgium	September 17, 1970	January 1, 1972
Brazil	November 8, 1978	January 1, 1981
Denmark	November 17, 1980	January 1, 1979
Finland	March 1, 1982	January 1, 1980
France	April 1, 1958	January 1, 1957
	September 8, 1970	January 1, 1971
Germany	August 23, 1958	January 1, 1957
	June 15, 1973	January 1, 1971
Ireland, Republic of	January 14, 1972	January 1, 1968
Italy	June 3, 1981	January 1, 1978
Morocco	December 19, 1980	January 1, 1984
Netherlands	May 8, 1968	January 1, 1967
Norway	May 6, 1983	January 1, 1986
Portugal		
Singapore		
Spain		
Sweden	July 14, 1983	January 1, 1981
United Kingdom	May 24, 1967	January 1, 1966
	July 18, 1978	April 6, 1975
	January 28, 1983	January 1, 1984
United States	December 18, 1962	January 1, 1964

Treaties limited to airlines

Country	Date of treaty	Applicable since
Iceland	April 29, 1975	January 1, 1973
Soviet Union	June 6, 1975	June 6, 1975

Treaties under negotiation

Treaties are in the process of negotiation with:

Canada	Initialed on September 13, 1984
Greece	
Korea, Republic of	Signed on November 7, 1984 and approved on June 17, 1986 (probably applicable from January 1, 1984 on)

How has Luxembourg evolved into such a freewheeling haven? A surprising advantage is the relatively small size of Luxembourg's banks—especially when compared with larger rivals in Switzerland. Luxembourg's banks do not have the global ambitions of many of the

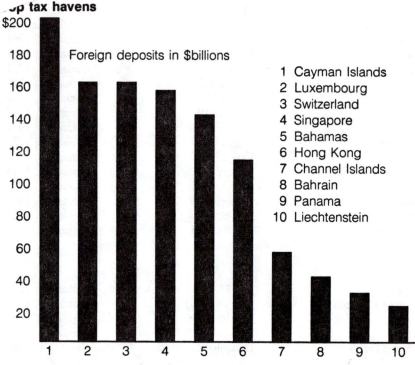

Foreign Deposits in Ten Leading Money Havens.

Top tax havens

Foreign deposits in $billions

1 Cayman Islands
2 Luxembourg
3 Switzerland
4 Singapore
5 Bahamas
6 Hong Kong
7 Channel Islands
8 Bahrain
9 Panama
10 Liechtenstein

Sources: IMF: Das Schweizevische Bankwesen; Walter Diamond's *Tax Havens of the World*, Matthew Bender & Co, Albany NY; FORBES estimates

Swiss banks. In recent years Washington has effectively threatened to investigate Swiss banks doing business in the United States unless Switzerland's authorities agreed to cooperate. A top U.S. financial regulator concedes that the United States could put pressure on Luxembourg banks, but that these banks are not nearly as exposed as the Swiss. Although trading in U.S. stocks through Luxembourg and Belgium totaled only $10 billion in 1986, compared with $40 billion of U.S. stock trading from Switzerland, the volume is growing rapidly.

The only way to crack Luxembourg bank secrecy is to obtain an order from a Luxembourg court. Foreign authorities cannot even ask for such a court order unless a depositor has been charged at home with an offense that is also a crime in Luxembourg and, moreover,

Figure 8.2. Foreign Deposits in Luxembourg and Swiss Banks.*

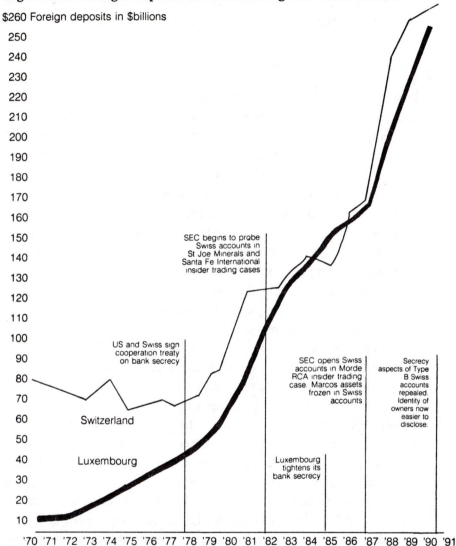

$260 Foreign deposits in $billions

'70 '71 '72 '73 '74 '75 '76 '77 '78 '79 '80 '81 '82 '83 '84 '85 '86 '87 '88 '89 '90 '91

*Restated to reflect current exchange rates—*Forbes* estimates.
Sources: IMF; Das Schweizerische Bankwesen

that relates to the account in question. At present the Grand Duchy is going to great lengths to facilitate the banking influx. Currently more than 120 foreign banks are clustered on Boulevard Royale— Luxembourg's Wall Street. In 1984 Luxembourg's parliament actually strengthened bank secrecy laws, mandating jail sentences for anyone making unauthorized disclosures about secret bank accounts.

INVESTMENT COMPANIES

Luxembourg's favorable holding company legislation has also had a magnetic effect on investment companies (such as Minorco, De Beers and Anglo-American companies' international investment holding company) and on Eurobond issuers. The majority of new Eurobond issues involve banks linked to the Grand Duchy, particularly in the European currency-unit denominated sector.

Luxembourg plays an essential part in the secondary market for Eurobonds. The local stock exchange lists over 3,000 Eurobonds issued by 1,400 borrowers from 50 countries in 17 currencies; most of them have paying agents in the Grand Duchy.

In the case of Eurobond issues, and where the holding company has a reasonable holding in the borrowing company (approximately 25%), such holding companies may grant loans without being subject to tax on interest income. To qualify for special tax treatment, the holding company may have no industrial activities of its own. This also excludes Luxembourg real estate deals.

Luxembourg legislation requires what might be thought of as awkwardly high debt to equity ratios. The most favorable treatment is given to companies making bond issues such as Eurobonds. In their case the ratio permitted is 10:1. But finance companies not issuing bonds are faced with a debt to equity requirement of 3:1, which, if operations are to be on any scale, would attract a fairly high subscription tax liability. In the Netherlands, Luxembourg's main European competitor for big holding company business, the ratio can be reduced to as little as 100:1.

The growing number of investment companies has contributed to the diversity in financial services available in Luxembourg. Investment companies now based in Luxembourg include some 481 mutual funds and unit trusts with total net assets of $23.8 billion. Among recent arrivals is Sumitomo Corporation International Investment, charged with international corporate fund management for Sumitomo Corporation, a major Japanese trading house.

The 1983 Tax Reform Law cleared the way for investment fund and mutual fund growth. The law drew a distinction between funds and holding companies, which are barred from investing in certain types of assets. Funds were then free to concentrate on areas such as financial futures, commodities, real estate, and venture capital. The three types of funds, the SICAV (a French acronym for variable capital investment fund), mutual investment fund, and other investment funds are exempt from income taxes and withholding taxes on dividends. They pay a one-time fee of LFr50,000 when organized and an annual subscription tax of 0.06% on net assets thereafter.

By creating a fiduciary arrangement or a Luxembourg holding company, a private restricted investment vehicle can be structured outside the supervision of the Luxembourg Monetary Institute. Luxembourg banks can offer fiduciary services that operate like trusts. Holdings that are restricted by law to the administration of financial assets are taxed on the basis of net worth rather than income. Like the funds, holding companies are exempt from withholding tax on dividends, and there is no tax on the proceeds of liquidation and no inheritance tax. They pay an initial registration tax of 1% of capital and an annual subscription tax of 0.2% of equity. A holding company can issue bonds amounting to ten times its capitalization.

CAPTIVE INSURANCE COMPANIES

Luxembourg has mounted a determined bid to attract captive insurers away from offshore re-insurance centers such as Bermuda, Guernsey, and the Cayman Islands. It has created an attractive tax environment for captive re-insurance operations. This, combined with high operating costs in Bermuda, has resulted in a switch toward Luxembourg. There are approximately 65 captive insurance companies at present in Luxembourg. The capitalization requirements for captive re-insurance operations are set at LFr6 million, considerably lower than the LFr50 million required for normal re-insurance companies. The solvency marginal requirements were also made very attractive to captives.

The minimum of funds to be set aside as a technical reserve was established at only 5% of annual net reinsurance premium income, as against the 10% minimum required of standard commercial insurance operations.

COORDINATION CENTERS

A coordination center is a Luxembourg company whose sole purpose is to provide administrative services to members of a multinational group. Administrative services include central organization and secretarial services, advertising and marketing services, collection and processing of technical and administrative information, liason services with national and international authorities, centralization of financial and legal services, together with any assistance or service directly or indirectly linked to these activities.

Coordination centers of multinational groups enjoy special tax status. These coordination centers are loosely based on Belgium's stability. Luxembourg companies that provide administrative services to members of its multinational group that are situated in at least two other countries. The ultimate parent must be resident outside of Luxembourg. Qualifying coordination centers do not pay corporate income tax on their profits but on 5% of relevant expenses.

Profit is determined on the basis of 5% of expenses incurred with a minimum of LFr1.5 million. If a coordination center acts as a clearing house for multicurrency invoices, then the profit is determined on 1% to 1.5% of the total amount of the invoices. For a coordination center having expenses of LFr40 million, the corporate tax payable would be: 40 million × 5% × 34% = LFr680,000, or approximately $17,000.

FINANCE COMPANIES

It is possible to use a Luxembourg holding company to act as a conduit to channel loans to a foreign subsidiary. The only tax incurred on interest payments from a foreign operating company to a holding finance company is foreign withholding tax. No tax is payable on interest received by the holding company from foreign sources.

A major benefit of using a holding company to provide finance to a foreign subsidiary lies in the ability to effectively shift the profits of a foreign subsidiary in a high-tax jurisdiction to the low-tax jurisdiction of Luxembourg. In other words, the interest or loan repayments to the finance company effectively reduce the foreign subsidiary's taxable profit, and the interest paid to the holding company is not liable for corporate tax.

The main tax objective of repatriating capital rather than income from the foreign operation is to achieve a lower rate of tax than would be incurred if income were repatriated. Loan repayments from a foreign subsidiary will be free of withholding tax in the foreign country and free of income tax in the hands of the Luxembourg holding company. However, in some cases the loan repayment could be treated as a repatriation of profits and taxed as a dividend by the foreign country, especially where the foreign subsidiary is thinly capitalized. An alternative is for the foreign subsidiary to repay or reduce its share capital where the Luxembourg company has financed the foreign subsidiary by way of equity finance. To easily facilitate such returns of capital, it is best to ensure when possible that the equity financing is done by way of redeemable shares.

INDUSTRIAL INCENTIVES TO MANUFACTURERS

While Luxembourg's tax treatment of holding companies is its most important tax-haven feature, the Grand Duchy also offers tax concessions to manufacturers qualifying under the various industrial incentive programs. Luxembourg's law on industrial incentives and its liberal tax policy are primarily responsible for attracting more than $500 million of direct U.S. investment. Some of the incentives being offered are:

- Tax free grants of up to 15% of the overall costs of building, equipment, tools and industrial research, and development for capital-intensive projects. Grants may run even higher for reconversion investments requiring large outlays for vocational training.

■ Interest subsidies of up to 3% on bank loans for plant and equipment, research and development, training, and recycling.

■ General tax credits on investments in fixed assets other than land and buildings, amounting to 3% of the total investment and total cost of new investments.

■ Land allotments. The government has the power to buy or expropriate the land for industrial use and to lease the land free at a nominal cost to investors.

■ Reorganization of insurance companies is tax exempt.

■ Taxpayers may select the declining balance depreciation method of up to 30% of book value or 30% of the straight line method, whichever is lower. The above percentages are raised to 4% and 40% respectively for research and development expenditures.

■ In special cases, companies implementing major industrial investment projects may apply for a tax exemption for up to ten years on a case-by-case basis.

■ Under Luxembourg tax law, the government may establish special relief so that taxpayers from abroad who take up residence in Luxembourg receive a tax deduction or exemption by a discretionary determination. These concessions may apply for up to ten years and may include additional deductions of losses exceeding the normal five-year period and reduction of the net worth tax.

■ State guarantees are available for credits to finance buildings and equipment, research and development, and training or re-adapting labor, up to 50% of the maximum amount financed by the credits. (Diamond 1986.)

An additional industrial lure is the recent introduction by Luxembourg of film production tax incentives in its attempt to make the Grand Duchy an important European audiovisual center. These will allow production companies to reduce their local tax liability by up to

30%. A novel innovation of these tax measures is that foreign companies with little or no taxable income in Luxembourg can sell their tax certificates to local companies, which can use them.

1992

Luxembourg's opposition to full economic integration is based on the fear of some of the consequences that may evolve from knitting together the EEC countries' different monetary systems.

The reason for this obsession with fiscal matters and opposition to harmonization of every sphere of the EEC's various national economies is self-evident to Luxembourg's bankers, who fear that uniformity will mean poverty. They see Luxembourg's prosperity as bound to the country's flexible regulatory system, stiff bank secrecy, and mild tax regime. Without these props, there is concern that the Grand Duchy's popularity as an international banking center could disappear overnight.

It has taken many years for Luxembourg to transform itself into a mature banking center. Initially just a convenient place for wholesale Euromarket business, Luxembourg has now diversified into private banking, fund management, and re-insurance. The financial services industry provides a comfortable living for many of Luxembourg's 360,000 inhabitants. A recent EEC commission report warned Luxembourg about becoming too dependent on its business.

However, as the pressure for union continues to grow, Luxembourg will find it increasingly difficult to resist. Tax is naturally the big preoccupation. It is in this area that the EEC seems determined to make Luxembourg conform. Withholding tax, various types of capital gains tax, registration tax, and value added tax are all absent from the Grand Duchy, but could be imposed in any harmonization scheme.

How Luxembourg profits from its neighbors' stricter fiscal regimes was made glaringly obvious in 1989. The imposition of a 10% withholding tax in West Germany led to a rapid outflow of funds. Some bankers estimate that over 50% of the DM70 billion that left West Germany arrived in Luxembourg. In addition, it is estimated that some Fr7 billion of French investment funds has flowed into Luxembourg over the last couple of years, partly because of the absence of a withholding tax on the dividends and bank interest of nonresidents. French authorities are said to be deeply unhappy, and in Bonn it looks as if the withholding tax could well be suspended. In Luxembourg the mood is defiant.

The solution put forward by Luxembourg bankers is simple. There should be a zero withholding tax throughout the European Community, which would be the easiest solution. If the proposal by EEC bureaucrats for a community-wide 15% withholding tax is adopted, it could lead to a rapid flow of funds from Luxembourg and have a devastating impact on the Luxembourg franc bond market.

Apart from the tax issues, the other concern for EEC officials is the ironclad banking secrecy law in Luxembourg. This is enshrined in Clause 16 of the 1981 Banking Act. Recently, the law was strengthened. By a special decree passed under special economic powers, Luxembourg has given legal backing to the administrative restrictions that have long existed in Luxembourg to guarantee confidentiality and privacy to banking clients.

For now, Luxembourg seems to have gained time on the issue of bank secrecy, and a decision on any EEC-wide withholding tax is still several years away. However, other changes could affect Luxembourg much sooner than the outcome of either of these issues. When the EEC announced its Undertaking on Collective Investment in Transferable Securities (UCITS) regulations, Luxembourg pushed through legislation incorporating it into its local law. This gave the country a head start on its neighbors and helped create a boom in investment funds in Luxembourg.

The UCITS makes clear that unit trusts or mutual funds registered in only one EEC country can be marketed throughout the Community. Over 500 funds are now registered in Luxembourg, with total funds running into tens of billions of Luxembourg francs. However, since March 1988, banks and other institutions have been ordered to place the effective management of their funds in Luxembourg—a costly operation—rather than continue to run them from the Channel Islands or the Caribbean.

Many tax havens such as the Caribbean and Channel Islands do not have the benefit of the UCITS regulations. As a result management companies are often unable to market their unit trusts/mutual funds directly from their bases in these islands. As Luxembourg offers universal marketing capabilities for mutual fund companies, it is becoming an increasingly popular location to register such funds.

9

Channel Islands

As a result of the special status attained by the Channel Islands in relation to the members of the EEC when the United Kingdom joined the regional trading market in 1973, the popularity of the Islands as a tax haven was considerably enhanced. But even before 1973, the Channel Islands of Jersey, Guernsey, and Sark had already been recognized as a leading European tax sanctuary because of their special ties with Britain, the many commercial facilities available, and the benefits of low taxation and easy incorporation.

The reward for establishing a holding company in the Islands is exemption from income taxes, wealth taxes, estate duties, capital transfer taxes, and capital gains taxes. Guernsey is less developed than Jersey, but offers slightly more attractive tax advantages. Both territories enjoy complete freedom from value added taxes, and excise duties are lower than those in the United Kingdom.

The two lesser known Channel Islands—Alderney and Sark—have both been the subject of some discussion on their relative merits of operating as tax havens and offering certain specialized services. Recent developments in the attempt to transform Alderney are discussed in the 1992 section. At present special arrangements only exist between the United Kingdom and Guernsey and Jersey while none of the other islands have any such arrangements, thus drastically curtailing the uses of Alderney and Sark. (There will be no in-depth discussion of these two islands as their usefulness as tax havens is extremely limited.)

When considering any of the Channel Islands, management should also be aware that there are no exchange controls over movement of currency in or out of the Sterling area, of which the Channel Islands form a part.

Companies registered in the Channel Islands are subject to local company law. They must be formed with limited liability. Registering a company in the Islands with a place of control outside has the advantage of attracting the low corporation duty of £500 per year instead of income tax. The authorities have to be satisfied that control and management are really situated outside, which can be as near as the island of Sark, where there are no direct taxes or company laws.

The Islands maintain a highly tolerable 20% rate of income tax. Individuals are allowed various personal deductions. Locally managed and controlled companies and trusts pay the standard rate, which is deducted from dividends payable.

Dividends paid to nonresidents by local companies are subject to withholding tax at 20%. This tax can be set off against the companies' liability for local income tax. Externally controlled companies are free from the withholding tax on dividends. Guernsey has the advantage over Jersey of giving tax relief on dividend income from abroad at up to three-quarters the standard rate. Thus, for example, dividends received from the United States by a Guernsey resident would be subject to the U.S. 30% withholding tax and then to Guernsey income tax of only 5% of gross income, a final tax burden of 35%. In Jersey the dividends would have U.S. tax withheld at 30% and then income tax would be payable at the rate of 20% on net income, a final tax burden of 44%. The boom in unit trusts based on Guernsey was at least partly attributable to this particular tax advantage. No withholding tax is suffered on dividend distributions to nonresidents. Nonresidents are also not liable for income tax on bank interest earned in the Islands, provided that this is the only form of income received in the Islands.

Table 9.1 summarizes the current position on withholding taxes. Individual tax rates are summarized in Table 9.2.

Table 9.1. Withholding Taxes.

Payments from the Channel Islands

Payments of certain types of interest and royalties by resident corporations to nonresidents are subject to deduction of withholding tax at 20%.

Payments to the Channel Islands

The Islands have no effective tax treaties reducing withholding taxes; in addition, relief may also be lost for underlying taxes if income is routed via the Islands. The following rates of withholding tax are applied on payment to Channel Islands corporations. They are given as a general guide; specific reference should be made to the tax authorities in particular countries to determine the actual rates of withholding tax applicable to any moment.

Country	Dividends	Interest	Royalties
Australia	30% or Nil	10%	Special rates
Austria	25	10	20%
Belgium	25	25	25
Canada	25	25	25
Denmark	30	Nil	30
Finland	25	30	30
France	25	45 or Nil	33.33
Germany	25	10	25
Greece	Special rates	46	10 or 25
Ireland	Nil	32	32
Italy	32.4	15	21
Japan	20	15 or 20	20
Luxembourg	15	Nil	12
Netherlands	25	Nil	Nil
Netherlands Antilles	Nil	Nil	Nil
New Zealand	30	15	15
Norway	25	Nil	Nil
Pakistan	15	45 or 49.5	45 or 49.5
South Africa	15	50	15
Switzerland	35	35	Nil
Trinidad and Tobago	24 or 25	30	30
United Kingdom	Nil	25	25

Table 9.2. Individual Tax Rates.

	Jersey	Guernsey and Alderney	Sark
Income tax	20.0%	20.0%	Nil
Social security contributions:			
Employer	5.5	4.8	N/A
Employee	4.0[1]	3.9[2]	N/A

[1]Limit per month is £1,026 for 1988 (£1,102 for 1989).
[2]Limit per month is £1,157 for 1988 (£1,248 for 1989).
Monthly income above limits is not liable to percentage contribution.

The Channel Islands are the most popular tax haven for U.K. investors and those with business or personal ties with the United Kingdom. Although Britain has no direct control over the Islands, it is disturbing (from the tax haven point of view) to find how sensitive the Islands are when it comes to relations with the United Kingdom. For instance, the Islands' governments make it clear that they will try to ensure that any loss of tax to the U.K. Exchequer is kept to a minimum.

The absence of any capital gains tax, capital transfer tax, gift tax, wealth taxes, estate duty, or sales tax makes the Islands especially attractive for investments in gold and platinum coins, which are most often held for individuals and companies by the banks. The absence of sales tax gives the Channel Islands one advantage over the Isle of Man. However, for persons wanting only a bank account and lendings in equities, the cheaper cost structure in the Isle of Man and the total independence of Luxembourg suggest there are better tax havens available. Setting up a trust or desiring to move money situated in the Islands is far slower than many of the other jurisdictions covered here as a result of the Islands being in a state of excess capacity.

Guernsey and Jersey have reciprocal double-taxation-relief agreements with each other and with the United Kingdom and France. They have no agreements with any other countries, except that Jersey has a restricted agreement with France relating to profits arising from air and shipping operations between the two countries. The agreement of each island with the United Kingdom provides that a business carried on in Guernsey or Jersey shall not be subject to U.K. tax unless it has a permanent establishment in the United Kingdom. Under the agreements, residents of the Channel Islands or the United Kingdom cannot claim credit relief in respect of dividends received from companies resident in another Channel Island, but such persons can claim unilateral relief.

ANTI-AVOIDANCE LEGISLATION IN THE UNITED KINGDOM

Because the Islands are so near to the United Kingdom, U.K. tax avoidance legislation presents the main deterrent for potential users of the Islands. In particular, Sections 478 to 481 of the U.K. Income and Corporation Taxes Act of 1970 cover the transfer of assets abroad, and section 482 deals with the migration of companies or the transfer abroad of trade or business by a U.K. company. It is mainly Section 478 that prevents the abuse of the Islands by those who live in the United Kingdom. This section states that its purpose is to prevent "the avoiding by individuals ordinarily resident in the UK of liability to income taxes by means of transfers of assets by virtue or in consequence whereof either alone or in conjunction with associated operations, income becomes payable to persons resident or domiciled out of the UK."

The U.K. Capital Gains Tax Act of 1979, Sections 15 to 17, deals with the taxation of the chargeable gains that accrue to nonresident companies. Broadly speaking, these sections bring into account for capital gains tax such proportion of the chargeable gains made by the off-shore companies as is attributable to a shareholder in the United Kingdom. These sections apply to persons who are resident or ordinarily resident in the United Kingdom and are domiciled there.

Section 80 of the Finance Act of 1981 deals with the taxation of chargeable gains that accrue to a nonresident trust, the settlers of which are, or were when the settlement was made, domiciled and either resident or ordinarily resident in the United Kingdom. This section provides for the taxation of chargeable gains when a capital sum is received by a beneficiary who is both domiciled and resident or ordinarily resident in the United Kingdom.

The Finance Act of 1984 introduced legislation to provide that a U.K. company that owns more than 10% of the shares of a nonresident company and is controlled by U.K. residents may be taxed on the undistributed profits of the nonresident company unless it passes certain tests, for example if it pays at least half as much tax on its profits, excluding capital gains, as it would if a U.K. resident.

JERSEY TRUSTS

Trustees of Jersey resident trusts are not liable to income tax in Jersey on income that is derived from outside the Island as long as beneficiaries are not residents of Jersey. Where, however, a beneficiary is resident in Jersey or the trust is in receipt of Jersey income other than bank interest, the trustees will be liable to Jersey income tax.

The principal attraction of Jersey and Guernsey trusts is that they do not allow an individual to divorce himself entirely from the ownership of assets while entrusting professional trustees to apply those assets in a manner of which he approves. This benefit ensures that the ultimate owner of the assets (settlor) has some discretion over his trust investments.

A number of people using Channel Islands trusts are concerned about the effect that any reimposition of exchange control would have. As a precaution, Channel Islands trusts can be established with a trustee in another jurisdiction, such as Switzerland, as well as with a Channel Islands trustee.

Apart from private discretionary trusts, substantial numbers of unit trusts or investment trusts are established in the Islands and offer the most attractive vehicle possible for portfolio investment by both nonresidents and residents of the Islands. Although some withholding taxes may arise in the countries where the underlying investments are made, the off-shore structure will help to relieve the total burden. It may further postpone any of capital gains tax in the hands of the unit holder.

Figure 9.1. Jersey Trust Example.

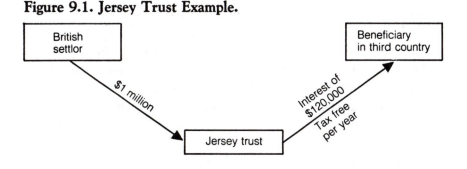

Substantial funds are also remitted to the Islands by U.K. residents who are working abroad for two or three years. If these funds were remitted to the United Kingdom, they would be subject to a tax liability. For many of these individuals, the interest in working abroad would be severely reduced if such a liability could not be avoided. In order to avoid tax, the worker abroad would have to follow the procedures below prior to taking up residence:

- The termination of his British domicile and residence;
- The investment of his funds off-shore; and
- The establishment of a trust.

The settlement of assets in a Jersey trust by the British worker abroad should be made on condition that liability for British capital transfer tax and capital gains tax will not arise. Funds will be invested in Jersey free of income tax and the individual or trustee can then make a distribution of income to the beneficiary abroad free of tax, on the grounds that it has a foreign source.

THE EXEMPT COMPANY

In effect from January 1, 1989, the corporation tax law was abolished, together with the corporation tax companies which were companies incorporated in Jersey, but not resident on the Island, for the purposes of Jersey tax. For 1989 and subsequent years, Article 123 of the

Income Tax Act provides that all companies incorporated in Jersey will be regarded as resident on the Island, so that the place where board meetings of Jersey companies are held is no longer of any relevance to determining the companies' residence for tax purposes. However, a new article, Article 123A, permits a company to be treated as nonresident for the purposes of the Income Tax Act, and therefore exempt from tax, if it meets the following conditions:

- No Jersey resident may have any interest in an exempt company, unless he is holding shares in a nominee or trustee capacity; and
- Exempt company status will be granted only if the full name and address of the ultimate beneficial owners of the shares are disclosed.

An exempt company is treated as nonresident in the Island, provided that it does not carry on any activities through a permanent establishment. An exempt company does not have to make a return of non-Jersey source income, nor is it required to file accounts. No requirement exists for the deductions of any withholding tax. Management and control of an exempt company may be exercised in the Island without incurring income tax liability.

A foreign incorporated company administered in the Island and not wishing to register as an exempt company would continue to be exempt from income tax in Jersey, if management and control is exercised outside the Island.

At present, there exist 18,000 exempt companies that contribute £9 million to the Jersey economy from the exempt company charge and generate significant tax revenues on fees paid to directors and advisors.

INCOME-TAX-PAYING COMPANIES

Thus, there may be a benefit in having an income-tax-paying subsidiary company where the parent company's country would tax subsidiary profit at considerably higher rates than 20%.

Other benefits include having access to Channel Islands capital a _ tax treaty relief (i.e., lower withholding taxes might be incurred where a finance company set up in the Channel Islands was receiving interest payments from its branch or subsidiary in another jurisdiction).

- Income-tax-paying companies pay 20% income tax on profits assessable to tax, but it is sometimes possible to reduce the effective rate to a very low level through management changes and payments of commission.
- Isolated capital gains may not be taxable, but capital gains arising from trading activities will be assessed to income tax at 20%.
- A withholding tax of 20% is deductible from the payment of annual interest.
- Income tax paying companies can be managed and controled in Jersey.

It should be noted that payments of commission, remuneration, fees, and the like made to a nonresident, such as a foreign parent, subsidiary, or associate, may be allowed, by concession, as a deduction against the income received by a Jersey income-tax-paying company from a foreign country operation, thus reducing the effective tax rate to a level substantially lower than 20%.

In certain circumstances, the granting of this concession can make a resident company the more attractive vehicle as it reduces the effective tax rate to well below 20%. Certain countries where the parent is registered, will not tax profits from a subsidiary, if the subsidiary has indeed incurred tax already, albeit at a low level (e.g., 20%). At present, there exist 9,000 income-tax-paying companies.

TAX-AVOIDANCE STRATEGIES

Off-Shore Mutual Funds

It is estimated that there are some 450 collective investment schemes of various kinds with Guernsey connections. Between them they hold worldwide assets valued at over £3 billion. Of these funds 139 are incorporated in Guernsey. The remainder are incorporated elsewhere and are either advised, managed, administered, marketed, or serviced in other ways by the local industry, which includes some 30 management stables and 70 management companies. Their clients are worldwide, although it is estimated that 100 funds are marketed in the United Kingdom. Local authorities are confident of retaining this market by achieving designated-territory status for the Islands under Section 87 of the United Kingdom's Financial Services Act. This will acknowledge adequate investor protection for potential off-shore fund investors. Guernsey has introduced its own Protection of Investors legislation and has appointed a full-time Superintendent of Investment Business.

Off-shore funds under management in Jersey have grown from £2 billion at the end of 1984 to over £7.5 billion in 1989. There is a total of 170 funds covering most markets, representing some 200,000 investors from all over the world. The issue of Jersey's relationship with the European Economic Community and the marketability of its investment products in continental Europe is an important one. The Jersey Fund Association will be working to ensure that there is no unfair discrimination against Jersey-based institutions.

The marketability of Jersey mutual funds has been a problem in the past. With the very strong possibility of Jersey complying to the UCITS standards, the marketability in the EEC of Jersey funds will be secured. The Channel Islands' special relationship with the United Kingdom and thereby with the EEC will determine the ultimate free marketability of their unit trusts/mutual funds. The problem arises from the EEC directive on Undertakings for Collective Investments in Transferable Securities (UCITS), which came into force throughout the Community on October 1, 1989. The directive enables unit trusts or mutual funds formed in any member state and which comply with the investment criteria laid down in the directive to be freely marketed in all EEC countries, provided they comply with each country's local marketing rules.

This free marketability of EEC-based funds puts funds based in Jersey and Guernsey at a disadvantage. Because the Channel Islands are only associate members of the EEC, its funds cannot be freely marketed in the Community. This has led to general retail funds being launched in Luxembourg, which has favorable tax laws for investors compared with other EEC members.

Some of the members of the Jersey and Guernsey fund-management industry have adapted to this challenge in a novel way by forming Luxembourg funds and subcontracting certain functions back to their Jersey or Guernsey offices. Although Luxembourg law stipulates that the custodian and registrar functions and certain administrative work must be carried out in Luxembourg, many Jersey and Guernsey fund management companies are able to work within those constraints to carry out portfolio management, investment advisory, and distributor functions for Luxembourg funds.

Captive Insurance

This activity is the speciality of Guernsey, because for many years Jersey company law did not provide for the registration of insurance companies. This changed with the passing of the Insurance Business (Jersey) Law during 1983, which enables insurance companies to be incorporated in Jersey. In recent years Guernsey has seen significant growth as a choice for locating captives, partly because of its geographical convenience and partly because the process of forming and running a captive insurance company in Guernsey is free of most legal formalities and bureaucratic interference.

In addition, the underwriting profits of a Guernsey captive insurance company are completely tax-free and the Administrator allows the reserves of a captive to be lent interest-free, which reduces the effective rate of taxation to a very low level. This is a further attractive feature of this type of operation, because it enables the necessary underwriting funds to be built up relatively rapidly. Jersey now offers the same attractions, permitting both freedom from restrictions and exemption from tax of the underwriting income of a captive.

In 1989 the United Kingdom's Department of Trade and Industry granted Guernsey designated territory status under Section 130 of the

Financial Services Act. This development acknowledges the existence of good local protection for investors in these products.

Private Investment Companies

The following example illustrates the specific and straightforward tax advantage of utilizing a private investment company. For a long time, U.K. death duty laws have recognized that a person who dies domiciled outside the United Kingdom is chargeable only in respect of property situated in the United Kingdom that he owned at the time of his death. For this purpose, U.K. assets are not included if they are owned through a Channel Islands company, because the foreign-domiciled deceased person will have been holding only the share in the off-shore company when he died.

Re-Invoicing

Re-invoicing or transfer pricing occurs where an intermediate company located in a low-tax environment (e.g., Channel Islands) is used by the parent company or affiliated group company to transfer/re-invoice these goods onto another group company in a large developed consumer market that has high-tax rates (e.g., Germany). By doing so, a large proportion of the profit on the sale of the goods is located in the low-tax environment.

This arrangement is well-known to tax authorities. Thus, it would be particularly necessary to ensure that the mark-up can be justified on an arm's-length basis and that the Channel Islands company does take certain of the commercial risks, such as those arising from loss of or damage to goods in transit or from default by the ultimate customer in payment.

Contracting

This is much the same as re-invoicing. Instead of a company in a high-tax country taking on a contract, a Channel Islands company does so. The Channel Islands company then subcontracts the work to the company in the high-tax country, at a profit to itself. This is of particular use when the place where the main contract is carried out has no local income tax on contractors, such as in certain developing countries, or where the parent company wishes to average out high and low tax rates and is unable to obtain a reduction in overseas tax by using a treaty country such as the Netherlands.

Licensing

Whenever a person owns a patent or similar property that is to be exploited worldwide, substantial tax savings in the royalty income may be obtained using the Channel Islands in conjunction with another country. In this case, the Channel Islands company owns the property and grants a license to exploit it worldwide to a company in a country such as the Netherlands. Royalties will flow from licensees to the Netherlands with the benefit of the reduced rates of withholding tax applicable under the double-taxation agreements. The Dutch company will pay the royalties to the Channel Islands, subject to the retention of a percentage in the Netherlands on which Dutch tax will be paid. The Channel Islands company will receive the royalties gross, because there is no requirement to deduct a withholding tax or royalties under Dutch law. Should the Channel Islands company be an exempt company, there is no withholding tax in the Channel Islands on payments to third parties.

Leasing

In the case of international leasing, similar benefits are received. A Channel Islands company will own the equipment to be leased. If the country in which the equipment is to be used levies withholding tax on lease rentals, a Dutch company can be interposed as the lease payments withholding will be greatly reduced. Normally, Dutch double-taxation agreements deal with lease rentals as if they are rates of tax. An agreed portion is taxed in the Netherlands and the remainder of the lease payments are passed on gross to the Channel Islands.

If the Channel Islands company is to pay rentals, then no withholding taxes apply, whether the Channel Islands company is an exempt company or an income tax company.

Financing

A Channel Islands exempt tax company may act as a financing company, borrowing money, the interest on which will be paid gross. The money is then lent either directly or, if withholding taxes are to be avoided, through a Dutch company.

A major benefit of a finance company in the Channel Islands is that it is beneficial to borrow money in the Channel Islands and then lend these funds to an affiliate and thus receive interest income at extremely low rates.

Ship Owning

A Channel Islands company can be used to own and operate a ship. Seeing that there are so many day-to-day activities to be undertaken in connection with running a ship, it would probably be advisable to establish an agency company as well. The Channel Islands company would then own the ship and employ the crew, and the agency company would arrange cargoes, ensure that the vessel was provisioned, and carry on other operational duties. By arranging the activity in this fashion, the shipping company would earn all the profits, subject only to paying a commission to the agency company for the services provided. As its income would be small, the agency company could be situated anywhere convenient to the ship owner.

Aircraft and Oil Rigs

The technique described for ships works for many other assets, such as aircraft or oil rigs. In a case where a tax saving could be achieved by using the Channel Islands, but substantial selling, management, or other activities are involved, the owner should consider splitting the activities so that the ownership of assets and, therefore, the portion of the income representing the return for the use of the asset is paid to the Channel Islands and the remainder of the income arising from arranging the exploitation is earned by another company.

Many international trading companies use the Islands for tax deferral reasons rather than outright avoidance. This technique has been used recently by oil exploration companies. Clearly, through providing this opportunity for tax deferral, low tax areas such as the Channel Islands can be responsible for encouraging new investment (such as oil exploration), from which other communities in Europe and elsewhere can benefit.

CONSIDERATIONS FOR INDIVIDUALS: RESIDENCE VERSUS DOMICILE

Generally immigrants who settle in the United Kingdom, on becoming resident there, will be subject to income tax on their worldwide income. However, proper planning can ensure significant tax savings.

Individuals who are resident but not domiciled in the United Kingdom are not subject to tax on foreign income that is not remitted to the United Kingdom. They are also exempt from capital gains tax on foreign capital gains that are not remitted to the United Kingdom and from capital transfer tax on foreign assets.

Therefore, it is clear that an immigrant to the United Kingdom should avoid being regarded as domiciled there for tax purposes. However, the immigrant should not sever completely his ties with his home country, since "interests" such as investments in his home country will be the deciding factor as to whether he is a U.K. resident or a domiciliary.

The Channel Islands is often a convenient place to transfer part of one's wealth (through the means of a trust), when leaving one country to reside or work in another. Many British citizens on their way or prior to their arrival in a new country—to work (e.g., United States, Germany, Australia)—deposit capital funds in the Channel Islands and are able to live off the interest in many circumstances tax free. (See Appendixes 2 through 7 for recent evidence of the Channel Islands growth.)

1992

Under the Treaty of Rome, the Channel Islands (whose external and international affairs are governed by the United Kingdom) would have entered 1992 as European territories whose external affairs would have been the responsibility of a prospective member state. Thus, they would automatically have been embraced as associate members of the EEC as and when the United Kingdom itself was admitted.

This prospect was not at all attractive to the Channel Islands. Over the years they had achieved conditions of considerable economic prosperity, largely by virtue of their attractive tax structure and tax rates. However, it then appeared that these advantages would be threatened by the EEC fiscal harmonization policy. Initially, it seemed that the harmonization directives would be extended to the Islands or, alternatively, that the Islands would be excluded altogether from the Community. This would have meant that they would have been excluded from the only feasible market for horticultural and agricultural produce. However, after long negotiations among the EEC, the U.K. government, and the Islands, agreement was reached on an amendment to the Treaty of Rome and on a protocol to the Treaty of Accession. Essentially, these exclude the Islands from all aspects of the Treaty of Rome other than those relating to free trade and movement of agricultural and industrial products, which treat the Islands and the United Kingdom as one member state.

Given that Protocol 3 (which excludes the Channel Islands from all aspects of the Treaty of Rome) can be changed only by the unanimous decision of the 12 member countries of the EEC, and given also that the perception of the Islands in the Commission in Brussels is that they are responsible jurisdictions that have not abused their privileges, the status quo appears to be an option open to the Islands and the best one available in the context of the development of finance business. It appears that the Islands will continue to attract more offshore business from the countries of the European Community without themselves being drawn fully into the Community.

Therefore, the Islands have now achieved a special status in relation to EEC countries, and there are many different situations in which considerable potential advantages may be obtained. However, this privileged position depends to a considerable extent on the high degree of internal supervision that both Guernsey and Jersey maintain. The manner in which the Island authorities monitor financial activities is fundamental to the preservation of Jersey and Guernsey as highly respectable and reliable financial centers. Consequently, the Island authorities will not countenance either residents or outsiders using their territories for evasive activity.

Efforts to Transform Alderney

The small Channel Island of Alderney is attempting to become an off-shore financial center, acting on an idea promoted by Douglas Calder, a local financier and director of Guiness Flight SARL. The president of the Alderney finance committee has approved the plan, perhaps in part due to Alderney's budget deficit of approximately £1,000,000. The neighboring Channel Island of Guernsey may attempt to curtail Alderney's plans, which is surprising in the light of Guernsey's mature and developed status internationally as a full-service off-shore finance center. If Guernsey was to block Alderney's limited attempt to create a small finance center, it is believed that Alderney would attempt to obtain approximately 10% of Guernsey's profits from financial deals and have these funds paid into an Alderney account. It is indeed ironic that Guernsey should want to block this plan, when at the same time it complains of overcrowding on its own island.

Alderney could benefit substantially as a new tax haven. An agreement with the United Kingdom could be signed allowing increased commercial activity in the island. Alderney, in a similar manner to Jersey and Guernsey, could benefit from a special status in Europe in 1992.

Thus, EEC proposed harmonization of withholding taxes and financial services directives do not extend to the Islands. For the marketing of financial services within the EEC Islands based institutions are treated like other "third-country" institutions. Section 87 of the U.K. Financial Services Act provides access to the U.K. market for Jersey and Guernsey based mutual funds.

10

The Isle of Man

The Isle of Man, a British island located in the Irish Sea between Great Britain and Ireland, is independent and self-governing. It has its own tax system that is completely independent of that of the United Kingdom. A double-taxation treaty exists between the United Kingdom and the Isle of Man.

The only direct taxation is income tax, which is imposed on individuals and resident companies. Individuals are subject to a standard rate of 15% on the first £8,000 of taxable income and 20% thereafter. Resident companies are subject to a standard rate of 20%, and their dividends are treated as a charge against profits to determine taxable profit. There is no capital gains tax, capital transfer tax, inheritance tax, estate duty, wealth tax, surtax, or gift tax.

Income tax is assessed on the worldwide income of Manx residents. Companies that are incorporated in the Isle of Man but not resident there are not subject to income tax. Investment holding companies, as well as shipping companies, whose income is derived from outside the Island and which are beneficially owned outside the Island, can obtain exemption from Manx income tax.

In February 1991 the Isle of Man pioneered comprehensive deposit protection laws equivalent to those in the United States, and United Kingdom. Deposits in Manx banks are now protected up to 75% of the first £20,000.

Insurance companies carrying on business in the Isle of Man are subject to normal tax on underwriting and investment profits. However, insurance companies licensed under the Exempt Insurance Companies Act of 1981 are totally exempt from the income tax, as is any insurance company whose entire underwriting risks are located outside the Isle of Man.

EXEMPTIONS FROM WITHHOLDING TAXES

A withholding tax of 20% in the form of a nonresident income tax is applied to payments of dividends, royalties, and rents by Manx resident companies to nonresidents. This does not apply to nonresident Manx companies, which are not liable to Manx income tax.

Since dividends paid by a company are allowed as a charge against the company's profits before tax, dividends are paid out of the pre-tax profits and thus there is no double taxation.

The following exceptions and exemptions are of significance:

- Bank interest (income or withholding tax);
- Dividends paid by exempted investment trusts to nonresidents are exempt from withholding tax. Thus, where such a company distributes all its income, there is no Manx income tax; and
- Exempted shipping companies are exempt from all Manx income tax.

Double Taxation Relief

Apart from interest on certain British government securities, which may be paid gross of tax, income from sources in the United Kingdom is entitled to relief from double taxation under the terms of the treaty between Great Britain and the Isle of Man. In addition, an individual may be entitled to make a claim to the Inland Revenue to have the U.K. personal allowance set off against the U.K. source income and to have further unilateral relief for Manx income charged on U.K. dividends and debenture interest.

Although no other double-taxation agreements exist, relief is still given for any income that suffers double taxation. As with the U.K., relief is based on the lower of the overseas rate of the tax or the Manx marginal rate of tax.

TRUSTS

Under certain circumstances, the income of trusts is exempt from taxation.

The Isle of Man's trust law is well established and well regulated. Unlike the law of Jersey and Guernsey, which is French-Norman based, Manx trust law is based upon corresponding U.K. legislation. However, there is one important difference: a Manx trust is permitted to accumulate income without any form of restriction. For residents abroad no U.K. tax is levied unless someone resident in the United Kingdom benefits. Moreover, there are no Manx stamp duties or taxes upon the formation of a trust and no Manx tax is payable on either accumulations or payments of income by the trust.

Trusts are used by expatriates to avoid local income tax in their chosen country. The advantage of off-shore trusts is that, once a capital sum has been put into a trust, it no longer belongs to the settlor. Most countries levy tax on a resident's worldwide income, but the capital invested in a Manx trust no longer belongs to the settlor, and neither does the income generated. Manx trusts also offer total anonymity, as no registration of either settlor or beneficiary is required.

Another efficient use of a trust is to avoid inheritance tax. If a person entrusts a sum for his grandchildren, it does not form part of his estate upon death. While the current Manx maximum is 80 years, the "lifespan" of a trust can be determined beforehand at the discretion of the trustee and can be tailored to suit the beneficiaries' tax positions. With a portfolio in a Manx trust, a taxpayer also avoids the tax normally levied in the United Kingdom on any capital gains when an investment is switched. The Isle of Man is ideal for individuals who do not need to make use of their capital invested in a trust.

An expatriate who wishes to return to the United Kingdom can set up a trust in the Isle of Man before leaving the country in which he is residing. By this means he can eliminate the amount in trust from his estate when he returns to the United Kingdom and protect it from tax until the benefit is realized by the beneficiaries, thus avoiding or deferring capital gains tax.

Exempt Trusts

A trust with a Manx resident trustee is subject to Manx taxation at the standard rate of 20% on income. However, by an exempt trust, the trust will not be subject to Manx tax where such a trust

- Is funded from sources outside the Isle of Man;
- Has no income arising in the Isle of Man (other than bank interest); and
- All beneficiaries are resident outside the Isle of Man.

Because of its nature, a trust does not normally trade, although it can hold investments and thereby form and own companies. The trust, in turn, may own trading companies or holding companies. This structure has many other advantages in relation to administration. A single holding company can be owned by more than one trust, thus preserving the ownership of shares in an enterprise in one name, but effectively allocating the ownership to different individuals in defined proportions.

Such a holding company can be exempt from Manx income tax under the Income Tax (Exempt Companies) Act of 1984, where the trust or trusts are exempt. This tax exemption applies equally to unit trusts (mutual funds).

An exempt company, unlike a nonresident company, may be managed and controlled and operate its business entirely from within the island, provided that it is owned by non-Manx residents and its sources of income are outside the Isle.

EXEMPT RESIDENT COMPANIES

Exempt companies are controlled and managed within the Isle of Man but have ultimate nonresident ownership. Recent changes to the taxation regime have extended the permitted activities of exempt companies, substantially increasing the opportunities available in the Isle of Man. Exempt company status requires that the trade or business not be carried out in the Isle of Man unless it is such that all receipts and income are derived outside the island or from other exempt companies or approved financial institutions. Examples of when exempt resident companies are most attractive would include international mutual funds, export-oriented consulting service companies, and international financing companies where profits are generated outside the borders of the Isle of Man. The exempt company is a very suitable vehicle for an international holding company and may deal in securities, land, ships, licensing, and most other investments.

When looking to create a new public company on the international stock exchanges one could resort to a Manx public company. Such a company would have the international credibility that is required. The exempt company provision in the Isle of Man makes special arrangements for public companies to have exempt company status, notwithstanding that there may be Manx resident shareholders.

NONRESIDENT COMPANIES

For the purposes of the Manx income tax, the residence of a Manx company is of great importance, since only resident companies are subject to the tax.

A company is deemed to be resident in the Isle of Man if the majority of its directors are personally resident and if the meetings of the directors take place in the Isle of Man.

Although it is incorporated under Manx law, a nonresident company is considered to be an overseas company and is taxable in the Isle of Man only to the extent that it trades or has income arising in the Isle of Man. If it receives dividends from a Manx resident company, withholding tax is applied to the dividend.

It is clear that a Manx nonresident company can provide an effective tax-exempt vehicle. If the directors of such companies reside in the Isle of Man and the board meetings are held there, the companies are liable to Manx income tax. It is possible for such companies to have their directors overseas but be administered from the Isle of Man without any Manx tax liability at all.

GUARANTEE AND HYBRID COMPANIES

The Isle of Man also offers two other forms of companies, namely *guarantee companies* and *hybrid companies*. The easiest way of understanding the importance of these two types of companies is to observe that most revenue authorities treat them in much the same way as a Liechtenstein Anstalt and that each can act both as a trust and as a company. The potential advantage can be seen in the case of a U.K. person who emigrates to the United States. If his guarantee or hybrid company is structured correctly, the U.S. authorities could deem it to be a trust, notwithstanding its corporate form. Thus, the emigrant would successfully avoid inheritance tax and control his U.S. tax liability.

Both the guarantee company and the hybrid company provide variable degrees of member control. The guarantee company has no stock or shares. The hybrid company allows for the shareholders to be a different group of people from the non-shareholder members. As such, the shareholders could be professional trust administrators, in whom all the voting and administrative powers could be vested, while the beneficial owners could be the non-shareholder members in whom all the rights to income and capital could be vested. By this means control is divorced from beneficial interest. These vehicles are, in fact, a range of trusts wrapped up in corporate form in which the beneficiaries may or may not exercise real control.

With regard to U.S. tax regulations in the context of guarantee companies, where the member has voting power but no stock, it would seem reasonable to assume that the IRS may well interpret membership by reference to the voting power rather than the nature of the participation. If the guarantee company has two classes of members (as can be the case in hybrid companies)—that is, voting shareholder members and non-voting shareholder members—this might very well weaken the argument against taxing the guarantee company as a corporation. In these circumstances, it may well be taxed as a trust, with the shareholders considered as trustees and the non-voting shareholder members treated as beneficiaries.

Even though guarantee and hybrid companies provide a fascinating tool for U.S. tax planning, it should be recognized that they must be handled very carefully and with precision. By careful structuring, their taxable status can be determined and they can be designed to achieve very precise objectives.

An example may illustrate this. Remember, where an individual is a nonresident of the Isle of Man, the income he receives is not taxable in the hands of the beneficiary. Where some of the beneficiaries are resident and some not, it is possible to arrange that resident beneficiaries receive capital not subject to capital gains tax and the income earned is given to the nonresidents. In Figure 10.1, a trust situated in the Isle of Man has parked its assets as a loan account in the company. The interest proceeds are used to repay the loan, thus converting the income to capital. The hybrid (company limited by guarantee with shares) is used to divert occasional amounts required by the client to a non-related channel. Trust A in the Isle of Man cannot receive any funds. Only Trust B is capable of receiving capital funds at the discretion of the benevolence company.

TAX-AVOIDANCE STRATEGIES

Manx Off-Shore Free Port

The Isle of Man's free port, the only off-shore free port in Europe, makes possible direct imports and exports outside normal custom procedures.

The free port, near Ronaldsway, allows guaranteed free movement of goods between the Island, the EEC, and non-EEC members. No duties are payable until the goods enter the country of final destination. The absence of customs formalities and commercial documents for control results in the simplification of international trade procedures.

Among the wide range of activities that can be undertaken on the free port site are several of particular interest to exporters and manufacturers who wish to extend their operations to Europe.

Figure 10.1. Isle of Man Trust Structure.

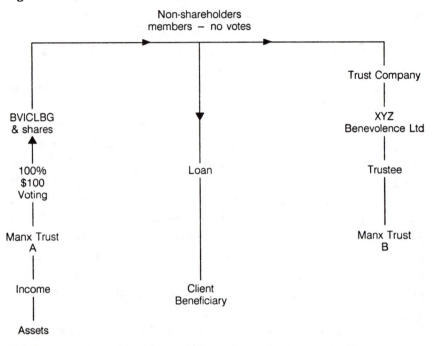

BVI Company accumulates income, but pays loan only when required
XYZ Benevolence is the settlor of Trust B

Apart from the obvious cost advantages of using free port facilities, businesses may obtain reduced insurance premiums because the goods are valued at their pre-duty price. In addition, traders may store goods duty-free for indefinite periods and enter them into the market when trading conditions are most favorable. Goods subject to quota restrictions can be stored pending the availability of suitable quotas.

The cost to companies renting or buying their own buildings can be substantially reduced by taking advantage of the various grants and loans offered by the Isle of Man government. Companies not wishing to buy or rent their own warehouses can use the public warehouse, which provides storage and transhipment facilities.

Anxious to attract commerce and industry, the Isle of Man government offers various incentives. Capital grants of 40% of the cost of new and improved buildings, plant facilities, and machinery are available. First year non-recurring expenses, the commissioning and running-in of equipment, and the cost of transporting equipment and key personnel receive a 40% operating grant. Grants for new marketing ventures, energy consumption, and micro-processing technology also receive 40% grants.

Since a major objective of the incentives and grants is the provision of work for locals, the training grant is set at 50%. Further, the government offers loans of 50% of the working capital requirement at low interest rates. Repayment does not begin until two years after the loan is granted.

For trading concerns there is a generous system of capital allowances that provide for up to 100% allowances in certain instances. There are also tax holidays, investment grants, lost relief provisions including group relief, share incentives schemes, and pension legislation, to name but a few of the many taxation measures available.

There are no exchange controls or taxes on capital gains, wealth, succession, or gifts in the tax system of the Isle of Man.

Collective Investment Schemes

Collective investment schemes authorized under Section 3 of the Financial Supervision Act of 1988 may be promoted to the general public in the Isle of Man, the United Kingdom, Guernsey, and Jersey under the terms of the Isle of Man's respective designation orders in each of those countries or territories.

The Isle of Man was the first overseas territory to obtain designation under Section 87 of the U.K. Financial Services Act of 1986. In order to obtain this designation, it was necessary for the island to satisfy the U.K. government that the law under which collective investment schemes are authorized affords equivalent investor protection. As the island is not a member of the EEC, the UCITS directive does not apply on the island, even though the Financial Supervision Act of 1988 is closely modeled on the English Financial Services Act of 1986, which took its inspiration from the UCITS directive itself.

Manx Companies

Manx companies can be used to avoid taxation under certain circumstances.

For example, a person who is a resident of the United Kingdom, but not domiciled there, would normally be subject to U.K. income tax on overseas investment income and to capital gains tax to the extent that overseas income or gains are remitted to the United Kingdom. As the Isle of Man is outside the United Kingdom for tax purposes, a resident non-domiciliary in the United Kingdom could avoid these taxes by interposing a Manx company.

Similarly, such persons are not subject to capital transfer tax, except to the extent that they own assets situated in the United Kingdom. Ownership of such assets through a Manx company can provide the individual with protection from capital transfer tax by ensuring that all assets owned directly by him are situated outside the United Kingdom. In another case, U.K. resident employees who are assigned overseas for at least 12 months are normally entitled to complete exemption from tax on their earnings. However, this is not available to self-employed individuals who work overseas for a similar period. A Manx company may be interposed to enable the individual to obtain the exemption by working for the company under an employment contract.

Within the island's tax-free climate the one issue that casts a slight cloud is inheritance tax. The expatriate investor who is not domiciled in the United Kingdom should not be liable to this tax, which is levied at 40% to depositors holding large funds. The problem arises with the building societies existing as branches of their U.K. operations, although it is the *situs* of the deposit which is important and the location of the parent company should be irrelevant. Provided the taxpayer is a Manx depositor and not a shareholder, and the account is transacted only within the Isle of Man and the deposit repaid in the Isle of Man, he should be safe from inheritance tax.

1992

The Isle of Man has a special relationship with the European Community. The Isle of Man is part of the Community's free trade area and follows EEC external trade policies with third countries. It is effectively excluded from all other aspects of the Treaty of Rome and has the right to set and collect its own taxes, except for the common external tariffs and certain agricultural levies.

With the approach of 1992 and European harmonization, however, the position of the Isle of Man as an off-shore center in Europe has been thrown into some doubt. The Island is associated with the European Community only through its position under Protocol 3, which gave it a "special" relationship with the Community under the United Kingdom's Treaty of Accession in 1992. Thus, Brussels is in no position to interfere with the Isle of Man's status. In the words of Bill Dawson, Chief Financial Adviser to the Manx government, there is no reason why harmonization should affect the Island's constitutional position.

Dawson's view is not universal in the Island, however. Concern stems from a more indirect threat. The low-tax centers that already exist in the European Community could, if they retain their low tax status, gain a competitive edge over the Island. The relationship under Protocol 3 enables the Island to trade freely within the community, but does not require a financial involvement with the EEC budget or a commitment to long-term harmonization.

The Manx government has set up a working party to look at the options for the Island and to monitor legislative progress in the European Community as it builds up to 1992. So far the working party has presented three possible scenarios. The first option is to retain the special relationship afforded by Protocol 3. The second option is for the Island to become the equivalent of a full member of the European Community, accepting the advantages and obligations of such status. The third option would involve amending or terminating Protocol 3, which would enable the Island to act independently, but would remove the ability to trade freely within the European Community.

The problems facing the legislators are immense, and until the European Community issues directives it is difficult for them to know which direction to take. The year 1992 means different things to different sectors in the Isle of Man; what is right for the finance sector might not be right for industry. Moreover, unlike the new financial legislation, the European single market is a much broader issue. The insurance environment in 1992 will be more complex than investment. As there are such widely differing regulatory and cultural regimes among the member states, harmonization in this field is not so advanced. Generally, it is believed that the single market will not wipe away many of the existing differences in the insurance market and that, although many U.K. companies are considering mergers of associations as their way into Europe, the need to consider the insurance implications of a step into countries with very different laws and traditions remains. Already there are some concrete changes planned that will, in particular, affect some larger companies.

Certain parts of Europe will be able to seek much better insurance deals. This stems from a new directive already passed by the European Community, which was effective on July 1, 1990. Companies now are able to place large non-life risks across European borders when the insurer has no office in the country of the risk.

The Manx government is preparing legislation to make regulations more user-friendly for other countries. The members of the finance community in the Isle of Man are so concerned about the potential benefits and risks of 1992 that they have set up their own fighting fund to employ a handpicked committee and legal counsel to put their case directly to the European Parliament should the Manx government move to a stance that would not enhance the viability of the Island's financial industry.

Both insurance and investment companies are determined to ensure that they have access to markets where and when they want them and that they will be in a position to offer their clients the best products they can develop for these markets. As the European legislation becomes clearer, the Manx-based companies will be able to react to it and secure entrance to the massive marketplace of 350 million people created by harmonization in 1992. (See Appendixes 2 through 7.)

11

Hong Kong

The British Crown Colony of Hong Kong is located on the southeast coast of the Chinese mainland. Hong Kong owes its high economic growth rate mainly to expansion in export-orientated light industry. It has also become a major international off-shore investment center, but financial services and tourism play only a secondary role in the economy. Hong Kong does not look upon itself as a tax haven, and only in certain respects can it be viewed as such.

Negotiations between the United Kingdom and China on Hong Kong's fate culminated in the joint Sino-British Declaration of September, 1984. Under that agreement, China will regain sovereignty over the territory, which will be given special economic status. On July 1, 1997, Great Britain will restore Hong Kong to China, and Hong Kong will become a special administrative region under the direct authority of the Central People's Government of China. Under the Joint Declaration, it is proposed that the social, legal, and economic systems of Hong Kong will remain unchanged for 50 years after 1997. Although some details still are to be settled, the commercial life and status of Hong Kong are intended to continue unchanged. Hong Kong will remain a free port, and it will establish its own trade and economic policies. Private ownership will be preserved, and Hong Kong residents will be allowed to travel freely. The Hong Kong dollar will be freely convertible into other currencies, but there is the possibility that eventually the Chinese yuan may replace the Hong Kong dollar. Real estate interests are to be protected by recognizing leases extending beyond 1997 and by allowing leases due to expire during or before 1997 to be renewed for 50 years after that date.

In spite of these assurances, investor confidence has been badly shaken. Investment by Hong Kong Chinese in real estate and business in the United States, Canada, and Australia has increased dramatically. Confidence has been further weakened by the redomiciliation of major Hong Kong companies, including Jardine Matheson to Bermuda, General Oriental to the Cayman Islands, and Sing Tao Publishing to Australia. During the 1990s it is likely that, while maintaining operations in Hong Kong, other major companies may look for domiciles elsewhere. Singapore or Japan could be the most important options for manufacturing groups.

Two-way trade between Hong Kong and China rose to $62.2 billion in 1990 from $15 billion in 1985. In 1985, re-exports from Hong Kong to China amounted to $7.5 billion as the People's Republic became more active in Hong Kong banking, finance, real estate purchases, and company take-overs. By the first nine months of 1990 total re-exports involving China were HK$78.2.

The consensus is that the take-over by Peking in 1997 will mean more U.S. trade with China and stepped-up investment in China by American companies, as the combination of China's massive labor force and Hong Kong's industrial experience will help many manufacturers to gain a price advantage over their competitors.

The increased reliance of China's industrial and manufacturing sectors on Hong Kong as a gateway to foreign currency and expertise indicates that by 1997 a *modus vivendi* will have been worked between the Chinese government and the Colony's Chinese community that will ensure Hong Kong's future pivotal role in international trade and finance. At present, China's need for outside capital is best served by such a vibrant financial and commercial center on its doorstep, which is most convenient in helping in the uplifting of China's impoverished economy by way of loans and new industry.

Paradoxically, Hong Kong's advantages as a tax haven arise in part from the fact that it is not a tax haven in the true sense of the term. Hong Kong imposes taxes on Hong Kong-sourced unincorporated business profits, personal income, property income, and interest at a standard rate of 15%. Foreign-sourced income is tax free. In order to attract deposits of off-shore funds, interest on foreign currency holdings with Hong Kong financial institutions was exempted from tax in 1982. Interest paid by certain priority borrowers, including public utilities, remains tax exempt provided it does not exceed particular levels, adjusted in line with current bank rates. As such, interest paid by financial institutions to nonresidents is not subject to tax. Interest sourced in Hong Kong is taxed in Hong Kong, but for a company that does not carry on a trade, business, or profession in Hong Kong, interest is taxed only to the extent that it is derived from the investment of other income sourced in Hong Kong.

Added to the low level of taxation, which is limited to Hong Kong-source profits and income, Hong Kong's freedom of exchange and its leading position as the manufacturing and trading center of Southeast Asia enable the establishment of many operations that have a "legitimate business purpose," thus avoiding the suspicion and adverse discriminatory treatment with which such operations in pure tax havens are often treated by the tax officials of high-tax countries.

It should be noted that no capital, wealth, capital gains, gift, or dividend income taxes are levied in Hong Kong. Irrespective of their source, dividends are not taxed. Dividends from foreign corporations are by definition non-Hong Kong-source income and thus exempt, whereas dividends from a Hong Kong corporation are exempt inasmuch as that corporation will automatically be liable for profits tax.

Uncertainty over the Colony's political future is its major weakness, although no drastic changes are expected until 2047. Tax-haven seekers might also consider the lack of double-taxation agreements. But it is of interest to note that, despite the 1997 threat, over 300 new foreign companies were registered in the territory in 1984, bringing the total of foreign companies in Hong Kong to over 2,000. The total of new companies rose by more than 10% to about 19,000.

It is easy to be alarmist about Hong Kong's brain drain and capital flight, but the problem is often exaggerated and little attention is paid to contrary evidence. The amount of money in Hong Kong's banking system tripled in the five-year period since the signing of the agreement to hand the Colony back to China in 1997. The year of the Tiananmen Square massacre, deposits actually grew by 19%. It is also apparent that despite continual discussion about an exodus of financial institutions from Hong Kong very little is happening. No one has announced a wholesale departure from the Colony. In fact one bank, the Bank of America, moved its regional headquarters to Hong Kong.

DOUBLE-TAXATION RELIEF

Although Hong Kong does not have any double-taxation treaties, Hong Kong nonresidents may claim relief from double taxation on the following basis:

- Where the foreign tax rate is less than Hong Kong's tax rate, a deduction may be claimed for half of the foreign tax paid.
- Where the foreign tax rate exceeds the Hong Kong tax rate, the deduction claimable is the amount by which half of the foreign effective rate of tax exceeds the Hong Kong rate. For example, assuming that a nonresident received income that had been taxed at the rate of 40% from the United Kingdom and was also deemed to have a source in Hong Kong, then the relief from double taxation would be calculated as follows:

Foreign rate of tax	40%
Hong Kong rate of tax	15%
Half of foreign effective rate	20%
Amount by which half of the foreign effective rate of tax exceeds the effective Hong Kong rate (20%–15%)	4%

The tax payable in Hong Kong on that income will be 11% (15%–4%)

BANKING

Hong Kong's excellent banking and financial facilities have played a vital role in developing Hong Kong's manufacturing center. Today, banks in Hong Kong are specialized in financing international trade, as well as domestic activities. They maintain extensive credit information and commercial introduction services for the benefit of their clients and for those wishing to establish business with Hong Kong.

Moreover, it is worth noting that Hong Kong has no central bank. The role of central bank functions, such as supervising financial institutions and managing official foreign exchange resources, are carried out by various government offices or by the note-issuing banks.

There are no exchange controls of any kind whatsoever. Therefore, funds can be moved into and out of Hong Kong at any time and for any purpose.

Bank loans and advances are available to all companies, local or foreign. Banks in Hong Kong have assumed the role of medium-term lender to establishments conducting business in Hong Kong. This type of lending usually takes the form of mortgaging land to the bank for building finance, and the loans are usually repayable over a period of three to five years. Banks are also prepared to grant medium-term loans for the purpose of machinery.

The Commissioner of Banking exercises prudential supervision over all banking institutions in Hong Kong. At the end of 1985, there were 143 licensed banks in Hong Kong, of which 35 were local companies. They maintained a total of 1,394 offices in Hong Kong. In addition, there were 131 representative offices of foreign banks. Bank deposits at the end of 1985 amounted to HK$367 billion and foreign liabilities to US$83.33 billion, as well as deposit banks foreign assets at US$101.17 billion. At present (end 1990) there are 168 licensed banks, 136 from abroad, with Japanese banks (30) having the largest foreign presence.

Deposit banks' foreign liabilities have risen from US$83.3 billion in 1985, to US$310.13 billion in 1989, to approximately US$403 billion at the beginning of 1991. Furthermore, deposit banks' foreign assets have risen in a similar fashion from US$101.17 billion in 1985, to US$355.64 in 1989, to approximately US$464 billion at the beginning of 1991.

USE OF TRUSTS

Hong Kong is not as popular as Bermuda or the Bahamas as a site for an accumulation trust because the latter two havens impose fewer restrictions. In Hong Kong, accumulations are limited to one of four periods: the life of the grantor or settlor, 21 years from the death of the grantor, the minority of any person living at the death of the grantor, or the minority of any person who under the terms of the trust would be entitled to the income directed to be accumulated if of full age. A trust that does not either create or receive income in the Colony escapes profits tax. One commentator suggests that the establishment of an accumulation trust in Hong Kong is recommended when a free currency market will prove an asset.

Hong Kong trusts can be set up with local trustees. There are rules against perpetuities, which can be circumvented. Trusts holding assets abroad have the advantage of paying no income tax or withholding tax in Hong Kong even if the absence of tax treaties makes their income subject to maximum rates of withholding taxes in, for example, the United Kingdom and the United States.

SETTING UP A BUSINESS

An entrepreneur can set up business in Hong Kong as a sole proprietorship, partnership, or limited company. Such businesses may engage in commercial, industrial, or professional activities or render services. The only requirement is a business registration certificate obtained from the Business Registration Office within one month after operations begin. A fee of HK$650 is due on registration and is renewable yearly.

Most often companies with limited liabilities are set up for carrying out a commercial or industrial venture. These companies are either privately owned or publicly listed on the unified Stock Exchange of Hong Kong. For tax purposes, no distinction is made between residents and nonresidents. As long as profits arise outside Hong Kong, no tax will be imposed. By setting up a manufacturing operation in Hong Kong and exporting the bulk of the goods to the Pacific, a company will incur minimal Hong Kong tax on profits, as these will arise mostly from foreign sources.

Furthermore, a transfer of certain allowable head-office administrative expenses by means of a charge to a local branch or subsidiary in Hong Kong would be allowed as a deduction for Hong Kong tax purposes. Other specifically allowable expenses include:

- Interest on funds borrowed and rent of buildings or land occupied for the purpose of producing the profits;
- Bad and doubtful debts;
- Repairs of articles, premises, and plant and machinery used in producing the profits;
- Registration of a patent or trademark used in the production of profits;
- Expenditure on scientific research and payments for technical education;
- Employers' annual contributions or premiums paid to approved retirement plans; and
- Donations to approved charities from $100 up to 10% of assessable profits after depreciation.

With the opening of the future market exchange in 1985 to replace the desultory commodities exchange, re-exports by Hong Kong soared. At present, air freight is the most popular means of re-export; the amount of merchandise carried by planes now exceeds $12 billion. Hong Kong is emerging as one of the most important freight forwarding centers in Southeast Asia.

TRADE AND INDUSTRY

The following are some of the factors which contributed towards Hong Kong's international reputation as both a major commercial

and financial center and a leading manufacturing complex within
Asia:

- There is no discrimination against overseas investors in commerce and industry, nor are there special conditions attached to overseas investment. Overseas investors and local businessmen are treated equally.

- Government economic policies are stable and are based upon a philosophy of minimum interference. The goals of free enterprise and free trade are consistently and faithfully adhered to.

- There is no exchange control or restriction on remittance of capital or profits into or out of Hong Kong.

- Corporate and personal taxation is low.

- Hong Kong is strategically located at the crossroads of Asia and has a fine natural harbor, the third largest container terminal in the world, a modern international airport, and excellent world-wide telephone, telex, and cable facilities.

- Hong Kong is highly regarded as an international financial center and offers banking services of the highest international standard.

- The labor force is intelligent, hardworking, and versatile. The cost of labor is low in comparison with other developing countries, and there is a good supply of high quality managers, accountants, engineers, and technicians. This is why many multinational companies are choosing Hong Kong for their Far East regional headquarters.

International Trade

Hong Kong has no controls on imports, exports, and re-exports other
than those arising from international obligations and those exercised for
health, safety, or security reasons. Import and export licensing formalities are kept to a minimum and licenses are not required at all for most
products. No duty is levied on exports. Only four groups of commodi-

ties, namely tobacco, alcoholic liquors, hydrocarbons, and methyl alcohol, are subject to excise duty.

Because Hong Kong does not collect any import duties, the entire Colony is a free port. A corporation that wants to conduct business without customs duties can also enjoy maximum secrecy if it organizes as a private company, since no annual report need be filed.

Each year thousands of businessmen come to Hong Kong to buy consumer products, such as garments, electrical appliances, electronic equipment, and toys. Their buying function covers merchandise produced not only in Hong Kong, but also in Taiwan, Singapore, the Philippines, Korea, Japan, and other Asian centers. Because profits tax in Hong Kong is levied on a territorial basis, that is, income not arising in or derived from Hong Kong is not subject to Hong Kong tax, the judicious buyer may wish to structure a buying company in such a way that it acts as an off-shore trading venture. In this way, the profits arising from buying merchandise not of Hong Kong origin can be exempted from payment of Hong Kong profits tax.

Depreciation allowances are favorable, as a corporation is allowed an initial deduction for plant and machinery of 25.5% for the first year and an allowance of up to 30% annually for wear and tear. The initial allowance for capital expenditure can be up to 35%. This initial allowance is in addition to normal depreciation ranging from 5 to 25%.

Trade with China

Hong Kong's trade with China increased dramatically when the People's Republic embarked on its program of modernization and opened special economic zones. Additional record trade is predicted for the future.

Hong Kong has become China's major trading partner. In addition to importing directly from and exporting directly to China, Hong Kong assumes the role of middleman, thus maintaining a most important link between modern China and the rest of the world. Approximately 98.8% of the goods imported from China to Hong Kong are re-exported. Of these goods, more than half are processed in Hong Kong and then exported.

The Chinese province of Guangdong borders Hong Kong to the north. The economies of the two regions have become closely linked. Since China began to encourage foreign trade in 1978, trade from Guangdong through Hong Kong has grown more than 100%, to the point where Guangdong's foreign trade accounts for more than half of its Gross Domestic Product. Guangdong generates approximately 80% of China's desperately needed foreign exchange. If south China is the engine of economic growth for the People's Republic, then Hong Kong provides the fuel. The benefits to Guangdong's 63 million people, as well as to China as a whole, represent a powerful force to maintain China's open-door policy.

The general opinion is that Hong Kong is and will remain the best base from which to serve trade with China. Many multinational companies have established offices in Hong Kong to serve this trade. In addition to Hong Kong's proximity to the mainland, these companies have recognized that a Hong Kong base can maintain close communications with headquarters around the world and employ the full range of Hong Kong services, from translation, legal advice, and research to transshipment and insurance that can be tailored to their needs.

The following developed countries have granted preferential access to their markets for a wide range of products exported from Hong Kong: Austria, Belgium, Denmark, France, Germany, Ireland, Italy, Japan, Australia, New Zealand, the United Kingdom, the Netherlands, Sweden, and Switzerland. (See also Manufacturing subsection.)

TAX-AVOIDANCE STRATEGIES

Financing the Entity

A business entity may be financed by either loan or share capital. Hong Kong does not impose any thin-capitalization or exchange-control restrictions.

There is an advantage to funding the entity via equity capital, as it may be disadvantageous to shift profits from a Hong Kong subsidiary to the home country in the form of interest. In this case, the interest paid would be deductible in Hong Kong. However, this would give rise to a slight tax benefit, given that the tax rates in Hong Kong are 16.5%. Conversely, the recipient of the interest may be taxed at a much higher rate of tax in the home country. In addition, interest paid out of Hong Kong must have tax withheld at the rate of 15.5%.

Some of the advantages of using debt funding are the following:

- Interest paid on a Hong Kong-sourced loan to a related company is tax deductible in Hong Kong.
- The loans can be freely negotiated in any currency.
- Gains or losses on foreign exchange will be treated as part of the Hong Kong subsidiary's working capital if the loans themselves were not used for the acquisition of long-term assets. If the loans were used for the acquisition of long-term assets, then any gains or losses resulting from foreign exchange will not be recognised for tax purposes.
- The 0.6% capital fee is not payable on loan capital.

The Hong Kong taxation system has not yet addressed deep discount loans or zero coupon bonds. This may facilitate flexible tax planning by the use of debt instruments to fund equity. The use of equity funding will maximize profits in Hong Kong, which will be an advantage given its low rate of tax. Profits may be retained or "parked" in Hong Kong, as there is no accumulated earnings tax. Although Hong Kong has no tax treaties, this can be overcome by using, for example, the Netherlands Antilles to provide some form of tax-treaty relief.

Holding Companies

Although Hong Kong is a popular off-shore financial center for the use of holding companies that fund the off-shore operations of a group, Hong Kong does not recognize the concept of consolidated entities for tax purposes. Thus, any group losses cannot be set off against the Hong Kong-sourced income.

One of the main advantages of a Hong Kong holding company is the avoidance of any capital gains taxes on the sale of subsidiaries.

The accumulation of world-wide profits by the Hong Kong company is facilitated by Hong Kong "source-only" taxation.

The advantage of a Hong Kong branch office is that the 0.6% capital fee payable on the share capital of a Hong Kong company is not payable by a branch. In addition, no withholding taxes are payable on branch profits.

The advantage of a subsidiary is that profits are taxed at a rate of 12.7%, which is comparatively low world-wide. If a branch structure was to be used, there is a possibility that the branch profits would be taxable in the country of residence of the head office. The fact that Hong Kong has no double-taxation agreements can be a serious disadvantage of the use of a branch structure. Further, the sale of the subsidiary's share will not attract any capital gains tax in Hong Kong. Thus, for example, the reorganization of group activities is facilitated when a Hong Kong subsidiary is used.

Off-Shore Finance Companies

An off-shore finance company may be particularly effective in reducing the impact of foreign withholding taxes on interest received. Hong Kong will not tax the interest received by the off-shore finance company. An off-shore finance company may be used to raise outside borrowings for the group as a whole, enabling it to pay interest free of the 16.5% interest tax that would have been withheld if the outside loans were made to the Hong Kong group instead.

The advantages of "treaty shopping" in relation to the withholding taxes imposed on interest paid are often crucial to the tax efficiency of the finance company.

Licensing Companies

A Hong Kong licensing company would be effective in shifting some profits from a high-tax country to a comparatively low-tax jurisdiction, while at the same time not compromising the legal protection afforded to the industrial and intellectual property. No prior exchange control or government authorization is required to transfer industrial and intellectual property to Hong Kong.

Where a Hong Kong company makes payments to an off-shore licensing company for the right to use patents and other intangible rights, 1.65% of the gross payment is withheld. Therefore, it is possible to minimize Hong Kong's 16.5% profits tax through the payment of royalties attracting only 1.65% withholding tax.

The transfer of other intangible rights to an off-shore company will result in capital gain, which is not taxable, or ordinary gain, which is taxable depending on whether the rights transferred constitute a capital or revenue asset to the Hong Kong transferring company.

Off-Shore Administration or Headquarters Companies

The use of Hong Kong administration or headquarters companies is common, as usually only 10% of the profit is regarded as being sourced in Hong Kong. Accordingly, that 10% alone is liable for tax in Hong Kong.

Profit-Reduction Techniques

A Hong Kong subsidiary or branch will seldom seek to reduce profits earned in Hong Kong because of the low rates of tax and its restriction to Hong Kong-source income. However, through payment of arm's length royalties and technical know-how fees, it is possible to extract profits from Hong Kong and effectively minimize the 16.5% tax liability.

Repatriation of Profits

Repatriation of a foreign subsidiary's profits to Hong Kong by way of dividend, loan repayment, or liquidation will be free of Hong Kong tax.

A Hong Kong subsidiary can make loans to its foreign parent company with or without interest charges. In practice, the Hong Kong Revenue will insist that an arm's length rate of interest be paid, provided that the subsidiary has not incurred interest costs for financing the loans to its foreign parent company that are higher than the interest income.

The purchase of assets by a Hong Kong company from its foreign affiliate also will not attract tax.

Manufacturing

In view of the low rates of profits tax, the development of a manufacturing enterprise should be funded through borrowings in the home country where the interest cost can be off-set against rates of tax that are normally greater than those of Hong Kong. The Hong Kong leasing industry is highly organized, so plant and premises may be leased on a financial basis. High rates of depreciation allowances on industrial buildings and machinery and full deductibility of expenditures on scientific research are incentives to encourage Hong Kong manufacturing operations.

The use of an off-shore licensing company to license the use of patents and know-how to the Hong Kong manufacturer can also achieve a substantial reduction in profits tax.

In order to minimize Hong Kong profits tax, products manufactured in Hong Kong could be sold at arm's length prices to an off-shore trading company for export, or the off-shore trading company might sell materials to the Hong Kong company at arm's length prices.

As a result of Hong Kong's shortage of labor, the use of China-based facilities and subcontractors has rapidly become an established feature of Hong Kong industry. An example of this is the Shenzhen Special Economic Zone across the border in Guangdong Province where labor-intensive manufacturing and assembly operations are able to make use of China's cheap and plentiful labor supply.

Hong Kong's hospitable business climate has attracted American investment. The United States is now the second largest investor in Hong Kong, after China, with total U.S. investment estimated at approximately $5.5 billion. The United States is the leading investor in Hong Kong's manufacturing sector, accounting for 41% of the total. Banks from the United States rank second in the Hong Kong lending market after the Japanese. As mentioned earlier, Bank of America recently moved their regional headquarters to Hong Kong. The U.S. investment banking firms Salomon Brothers and Morgan Stanley have active Hong Kong offices, too.

12

Gibraltar

Gibraltar is a British Crown Colony, approximately two square miles in area, located in southern Spain at the western entrance to the Mediterranean Sea. Gibraltar is a full member of the European Economic Community by virtue of its relationship with the United Kingdom. Gibraltar lies just west of Spain's Costa del Sol, a popular point of emigration for many Britons. Gibraltar is close to both the financial centers of Europe and North Africa, and it offers convenient transportation facilities and modern communications services.

Gibraltar is led by a Governor who represents the British Crown. On most matters of state, the Governor acts according to the wishes of a nine-member Council. The Governor is also advised by an eight-member Council of Ministers, which functions as a cabinet. The Gibraltar House of Assembly exercises legislative power. The Assembly consists of fifteen elected members, with the Attorney General and the Financial and Development Secretary serving as ex officio members. The Mayor of Gibraltar is elected by the members of the Assembly. Under its 1969 Constitution, Gibraltar has full control over its internal affairs, but ceded responsibility for external affairs, defense, and internal security to Great Britain. Gibraltar law is based on English common law and statutes, modified by local statutes and ordinances. The Gibraltar pound is on par with the pound Sterling and there are no exchange controls.

The restoration of a peaceful border with Spain has led to rapid growth in both financial activities and tourism. Gibraltar has asserted its role as a financial center by enacting legislation to make the jurisdiction attractive for international financial planners. One indication of this development is the establishment of branch representatives of a number of major international banks. The Gibraltar free port has benefited from the reopening of the Suez Canal. The port serves as a port of call for international shipping, offers repair facilities, and handles some transit trade.

The Gibraltar government actively intervenes in the economy and assists in a program of investment in infrastructure. The Gibraltar economy has grown at or close to 12% since 1988. Its unemployment rate of 2% and its inflation rate of 4.2% contrast markedly with the Spanish economy, which suffers from 30% unemployment and one of the lowest wage rates in Europe. However, this very contrast offers an opportunity for manufacturers, who can locate a plant in the Spanish industrial zone, take advantage of regional relocation incentives and favorable wage rates, and manage the facility from Gibraltar.

Today, the main focus of growth is in banking. In 1988, assets of Gibraltar banks grew by 100% and employment by 3%. Whatever else may remain for the European Community to decide, banking is now well on the way to a single European market. As a member of the Community, Gibraltar is in an excellent position for growth.

DOUBLE-TAXATION TREATIES

There are no double-taxation treaties between Gibraltar and any other country. However, Gibraltar and the United Kingdom have a reciprocal agreement under which relief in the form of a tax credit is given by one country if tax is paid in the other. There is also a modified form of this scheme in place with certain Commonwealth countries.

BANKING

The Banking Ordinance of 1982 regulates the licensing and conduct of banking in Gibraltar. Licensing and control is exercised by a Commissioner of Banking, who is advised by the Banking Advisory Committee, a statutory body. The supervision of licensed institutions is undertaken by the Banking Supervisor, who also assesses applications for banking licenses and reports to the Committee.

There are two classes of license for bank operation: Class A and Class B. Each is issued in full or limited form.

The full Class A license is issued to a bank undertaking business with Gibraltarians or residents of Gibraltar. Such banks can also undertake all types of international banking business. There is also a limited Class A license for deposit-taking institutions transacting business in the local market.

The Class B license entitles a bank to deal only with customers who are not Gibraltarians or residents of Gibraltar.

The paid-up share capital and reserves required for a full Class A or Class B license is £1,000,000 (or the equivalent in foreign currency). The minimum capital and reserves required for a limited Class A or Class B license is £250,000 (or the foreign currency equivalent). The number of banks represented has risen to 30, while their total assets rose by 70 percent in 1988 alone to close to $2 billion.

As a member of the European Community, Gibraltar can issue a license identical to one issued by the Bank of England. The advantage to the Gibraltar license is that it is less expensive, faster to obtain, and subject to less bureaucratic interference, while still meeting a high standard.

Any bank setting up on Gibraltar must have a physical presence. There must be at least two persons resident in Gibraltar and approved by the Banking Supervisor, each with sufficient banking expertise to manage the business of the bank. The Banking Supervisor will allow the managers to live in the Spanish hinterland provided that this is within travelling distance, to enable them to be present on a daily basis, during banking hours. There are wide powers for the protection of depositors and the regulation of capital reserves and business of the bank. Gibraltar is encouraging applications.

Banking secrecy is a high priority in Gibraltar. However, since 1988 Gibraltar law allows efforts to recover the proceeds of drug trafficking, similar to criminal-recovery laws in other tax-haven jurisdictions. The Gibraltar law gives the government the power to trace, freeze, and confiscate the proceeds of the drug trade.

Gibraltar provides a convenient haven for the thriving expatriate community in Spain, which adjoins it, particularly now that the commuting channels have been re-opened. As many as 250,000 Britons own property and live much of the year in Spain's nearby Costa del Sol. They can personally supervise their financial affairs, without lengthy correspondence or the risk of postal delays. Gibraltar offers familiar major international banks in addition to Gibraltar banks. Given Gibraltar's traditional links with the British people and its proximity to Europe, Africa, and the Middle East, Gibraltar is well placed to provide banking facilities for expatriates in many countries. At end-1987 total banking deposits were £480.6 million. By March 1990 this figure had climbed to £1,350 million of which £1,090 million are deposits from nonresidents.

EXEMPT COMPANIES

Gibraltar's dream of becoming a financial center and tax haven to rank alongside the Channel Islands, the Isle of Man, and Luxembourg date to 1967. Under the Companies (Taxation and Concessions) Ordinance, three categories of exempt Gibraltar companies were introduced: those resident in Gibraltar, those nonresident, and branches of foreign companies. Provided certain formalities are followed, exempt companies are not subject to income tax at the standard rate of 35%.

Whether a company is trading or merely holding investments, exempt status places it outside the Gibraltar tax net. The Gibraltar authorities will not levy value added, capital gains, or capital transfer taxes, nor will it tax bank interest earned in Gibraltar. There is no income tax liability on rental income, no estate or stamp duties, and no stamp duty on the transfer of documents for anyone buying company shares.

The Gibraltar exempt company is the most commonly used vehicle for clients requiring an off-shore company.

Gibraltar exempt companies can carry on business in any part of the world. The Ordinance makes Gibraltar an ideal forum and domicile for the establishment of companies engaged in varying types of business activities, including:

- Holding and investment activities;
- Trading and re-invoicing;
- Import-export and international trading;
- Agency and commission work;
- Management services;
- Shipping;
- Property holding and transactions;
- Captive insurance and re-insurance; and
- Patent-holding and receipt of royalties and license fees.

The conditions for obtaining Tax Exempt status, which is given for a period of 25 years, are that the Company may not be owned by nor transact any business with Gibraltarians or residents of Gibraltar and that it hold a valid exemption certificate.

Application for an exemption certificate must be made in writing to the Financial and Development Secretary and must be accompanied by references from a bank and a recognized lawyer or qualified accountant concerning the ultimate beneficial owners of the company and the company's future activities. The law ensures total secrecy in respect of this information.

An auditor must certify annually before the 30th of June in each year to the Commissioner of Income Tax that no Gibraltarian is ultimately beneficially entitled to the shares and that there has been general compliance with the legislation. For this purpose, it will be necessary for the company's books and records to be inspected, and certain written confirmation may be sought in this connection. The company's annual accounts do not have to be filed for public inspection or with any authority.

The Gibraltar exempt company differs in one significant aspect from Channel Island and Isle of Man nonresident companies, in that management and control may be located in Gibraltar and any interest accruing on a bank account in Gibraltar will be free from Gibraltar income tax. Recent developments in legislation worldwide are making it increasingly important for a company to have an indisputable location for control. Thus, the ability to provide day-to-day direction of a company's operations from Gibraltar can prove to be considerably advantageous from both the taxation and commercial viewpoint.

QUALIFYING COMPANIES

A qualifying company is used in those situations where a foreign jurisdiction requires that a certain percentage of tax on profits has been levied and paid. In those countries this requirement would not be satisfied by a Gibraltar exempt company because no tax is payable in Gibraltar on its profits.

Therefore, the Income Tax (Amendment) Ordinance of 1983 introduced reduced rates of taxation on the profits of certain qualifying companies and similarly reduced rates of withholding tax on interest, directors' fees, and dividends paid to nonresidents of Gibraltar by such companies.

When a Qualifying Certificate is issued, tax is charged on profits at the following rates:

- Income not remitted to Gibraltar: 2%; and
- Income remitted to Gibraltar: 17%

The conditions for obtaining a qualifying company certificate are the same as those for obtaining exempt company status, except that the paid-up share capital must be at least £1,000 and a deposit of £1,000 must be lodged with the government of Gibraltar as security against future taxes.

A single, one-time fee of £250 is payable on incorporation.

HYBRID COMPANY

A third type of company used in Gibraltar for off-shore tax planning purposes is the hybrid company. A hybrid company issues shares but is limited by guarantee. This type of company was abolished in the United Kingdom pursuant to the 1980 Companies Act, but is legal in Gibraltar. Hybrid companies are popular for trusts because they are flexible and provide the investor with confidentiality. A hybrid company may be established by three classes of members: (1) shareholders whose identity is disclosed to the Registrar and who own the shares of the minimum paid-up capital of 100 Gibraltar pounds and get a 5% return on same, (2) voting members who remain anonymous and who award benefits at their discretion, and (3) beneficiaries whose names are not subject to disclosure. A guardian may be named in the articles of association for further protection of the assets. Additional requirements for a Gibraltar hybrid company are the requirement for consent in using the word "trust" or "trustee" in the situs and at least one Gibraltar resident director and a person qualified to exercise legal authority.

TRUSTS

Unlike Spanish law, Gibraltar law is based on Anglo-Saxon legal concepts and recognizes and gives full legal effect to the concept of a trust. The Trustee Ordinance, the main legislation governing trusts, is based on the English legislation incorporated in the Trustee Act of 1893. There have been certain amendments to the legislation, and the Variation of Trusts Act of 1958 applies to Gibraltar.

The concept of a discretionary trust is known and widely applied in Gibraltar and the provisions of the Perpetuities and Accumulations Act of 1964 in England now apply with some amendments. The perpetuity period is ninety-nine years and the accumulation period now stands at a life in being plus ninety-nine years.

For trusts in which Gibraltarians or residents of Gibraltar are excluded from being beneficiaries, income of the trust may be exempted from Gibraltar tax even if the trustees are resident in Gibraltar. A further requirement is that the income of the trust accrue or be derived outside Gibraltar or, if received in Gibraltar, would not be liable to tax if received directly by the beneficiary. Exemption has also been granted from estate duty in respect of interests held by nonresidents in Gibraltar trusts.

The income of a trust created by a nonresident of Gibraltar with nonresident beneficiaries is exempt from Gibraltar taxes even if the trustee is resident in Gibraltar. The high degree of flexibility means that settlements can be drawn up to suit the individual requirements of each case.

No information about Gibraltar trusts is required to be filed with any official Registry. Accordingly, the existence of a trust and the identity of the settlor, the beneficiaries, and the protector, if any, are known only to the trustees.

TAX-AVOIDANCE STRATEGIES

Collective Investments Schemes

One area of particular interest for financial institutions in Gibraltar is that of collective investments schemes. The introduction of legislation will ensure that Gibraltar complies with the EEC directives relating to these schemes, commonly known as "UCITS." This will mean that Gibraltar will be one of only a few financial centers in the European Community able to take advantage of the UCITS directive.

In this area of business, Gibraltar's main competitor in the EEC will be Luxembourg. Although more established, Luxembourg is at a disadvantage in certain respects. Gibraltar is a common law jurisdiction, whereas Luxembourg has a civil law system. Many professionals agree that Gibraltar has a less complex and more flexible system of law for the setting up and documentation of collective investment schemes, and the legal system is improved by the more up-to-date and effective laws relating to investor protection now being enacted. Luxembourg has a waiting list for the establishment of such funds and delays in setting up can amount to more than a year.

Gibraltar enjoys a cost advantage over Luxembourg in terms of staff overheads, but Luxembourg is a more central location within Europe, being immediately adjacent to Germany, France, Belgium, and Holland. There is no income tax on mutual funds situated in Gibraltar or withholding tax on distribution therefrom. There is, however, an income tax on the investment manager.

The investment manager may be a qualifying company. This will limit Gibraltar income tax to 2% of the net income of the company whether earned inside or outside of Gibraltar or 18% of net income remitted to Gibraltar. Each qualifying company must make a £1,000 deposit on account with tax authorities and make a one-time tax payment of £250 for its initial qualifying certificate.

Activities conducted outside of Gibraltar are subject to taxation in the jurisdiction in which the business takes place. Sales activities and broker and dealer transactions will be taxable outside of Gibraltar. The impact of such taxation is not substantial.

Ship Registration

Using Gibraltar as a port of registry has increased appreciably in recent years in terms of tonnage figures. A person of any nationality can arrange for a craft to be registered under the ownership of a Gibraltar exempt company. In addition to benefiting from the tax concessions, they are able to fly the British Red Ensign and so enjoy the privileges and protection of the British Flag, since Gibraltar is part of the U.K. Registry.

Other advantages of registering a vessel in Gibraltar include no value added tax, no import duty if the vessel is not based in Gibraltar, no annual tonnage tax, and no tax on the sale of the vessel.

INTERNATIONAL TAX PLANNING

Qualifying companies have a unique status in the world of international tax planning. The Netherlands tax authorities recently ruled that a participation exemption may apply to dividends and to capital gains of a Gibraltar qualifying company that is a subsidiary of a Netherlands corporation if it pays tax at the rate of 3% in Gibraltar. As a result, a Netherlands company, which holds more than 25% of the shares of a Gibraltar company, will not be subject to corporate tax in the Netherlands if such dividends are paid out of income that was subject to 3% tax in Gibraltar. The Netherlands Company may not hold these shares as a portfolio investment. The subsequent sale of the shares in the Gibraltar qualifying company would, under the participation exemption, also be exempted from corporate tax in the Netherlands.

The key for Gibraltar is to attract the main stream of off-shore financial structuring work, which makes up the bulk of business handled in the Channel Islands and the Isle of Man. Such work provides high employment and demands legal, accountancy, and other professional skills. The Isle of Man has successfully penetrated this market and has become a first division member without question.

The Channel Islands have reached saturation point because of their geographical size and inability to house any more workers. Future growth of businesses located in the Channel Islands is forcing many firms to base their expansion in another jurisdiction. So far, the Isle of Man has been the largest beneficiary, but Gibraltar should be able to attract part of the overspill.

A critical advantage enjoyed by Gibraltar over Jersey and Guernsey is their trust laws. The Channel Islands have statutory trust laws, whereas Gibraltar relies on common law, which is far superior for trust work. Gibraltar should be able to obtain substantial trust business where large growth prospects exist.

Some forms of complex financial planning involve the use of companies limited by guarantee and hybrid companies that have both shareholders and members. The Isle of Man, Gibraltar, Cyprus, and the British Virgin Islands are the primary jurisdictions where such entities may be formed and administered. Presently, the Isle of Man has dominated such work, but Gibraltar has all the ingredients to claim its share.

TAX CONSIDERATIONS FOR THE U.S. INVESTOR

Gibraltar may be used to substantial benefit by U.S. corporations wishing to gain access into the European market; as a result of Gibraltar's inherent relationship in the EEC it has a benefit over other off-shore centers/tax havens as U.S. corporations will not have to pay customs or import duties on entering the European market with their product.

A new piece of legislation is currently being enacted as an amendment to the Bankruptcy Ordinance. This move may attract many American investors as it will mean that a trust can be set up and transfers into that trust, which are made when the trustee is solvent cannot be defaulted by a creditor in a bankruptcy proceeding. This could prove to be popular with American professionals, whose constant fear is that by some small mistake or natural consequence, they will find themselves being sued into bankruptcy. Therefore, a doctor could settle a proportion of his assets into a trust, which will most likely have no tax advantage, but he will be safe in the knowledge that those assets cannot be taken by a creditor.

1992

Gibraltar is a full member of the EC (unlike Jersey, Guernsey, and the Isle of Man) by virtue of Paragraph 4 of Article 227 of the European Economic Community Treaty, which provides that the Treaty shall (with certain exceptions) apply to "European territories for whose external relations a Member State is responsible."

In general, therefore, Gibraltar is treated as a part of the member state of the United Kingdom. As such, Gibraltar must comply with whatever Community agreements are adopted by the United Kingdom, as the European Commission will not afford special treatment to separate parts of a member state. The government of Gibraltar does make representations to the U.K. government to safeguard Gibraltar's interests when the United Kingdom is considering new EC edicts.

Gibraltar's special circumstances vis-à-vis the United Kingdom were taken into account on accession, and Article 28 of the Act of Accession granted three derogations. Gibraltar is not required to comply with Community rules on:

■   Common customs tariff;

■ Common agricultural policy; or

■ Harmonization of turnover taxes (notably value added tax)

The detailed provisions of the various EC treaties were adopted in Gibraltar by the passage of the European Communities Ordinance in 1972.

The two major factors influencing the present development of Gibraltar's economy were the enactment of the original Companies (Taxation and Concessions) Ordinance in 1967 and the full opening of the land frontier with Spain in 1985. The first marked the beginning of Gibraltar's life as an off-shore finance centre. The second made Gibraltar more readily accessible to those wishing to benefit from its facilities, many of whom are foreign residents of the neighboring area of Spain.

While the Madeira and Dublin Free Trade Zones depend on special concessions, Gibraltar's position is inherent in the basic terms of its membership of the EC. Gibraltar's relationship to the EC is fundamentally different from that of Madeira, the Channel Islands, and the Isle of Man because of the political circumstances when Gibraltar joined in 1973. Those circumstances have now changed, but Gibraltar's membership terms cannot be changed unilaterally by either side.

Gibraltar will benefit from 1992 by being able to give corporations and individuals a rapid response to their needs and problems and at the same time implementing these responses economically because of its small size.

The government is also willing to give as much help as possible to encourage new trade. In August 1989, an amendment to the Income Tax Ordinance allowed the government to change tax laws and allowances without the need for a fledged finance bill.

It is clear that Gibraltar is well on its way to becoming a leading player in the international off-shore marketplace. The latest figures show that it is now host to 18,000 holding companies as well as listing Barclays Bank, Royal Bank of Scotland, Riggs National Bank of Washington, D.C. At present commercial bank deposits are £1.5 billion.

13

Madeira

Madeira is an island district of Portugal, located in the Atlantic Ocean some 400 miles west of Morocco. Its low labor costs, hotel network, and positioning between Africa, Europe, and the Americas are an important attraction. The most significant aspects of Madeira as a tax haven are the exemptions from Portuguese tax and the incentives offered to qualifying companies in the Madeira Free Trade Zone.

Portugal is a high-tax country. The current corporate tax rate is 36.5% to which is added a 10% municipal surcharge. The current maximum personal tax rate is 40% to which are added substantial social security premiums. By contrast, the special arrangements made for the Madeira Free Trade Zone provide for tax exemptions for Madeira-based "off-shore" companies until the year 2011.

Madeira has its own government and legislative assembly. The regional government of Madeira is not responsible for national defense or foreign affairs. Madeira has its own regional budget, but the national budget is a matter for the central government. As a practical matter, the regional government is financially dependent on the mainland, but it maintains a great deal of autonomy in relation to the region's day-to-day activities.

The regional government of Madeira has worked with the central government for some years to persuade it to approve the legislation necessary for Madeira to operate as a tax haven. All legislation applicable to Madeira has been approved by the central government. This legislation has also been approved by the European Economic Community.

Since the central government is responsible for all national legislation, including Portuguese tax legislation, potential problems may arise from time to time. By definition, any change in Portuguese law will apply to Madeira. Unfortunately, those responsible for introducing and implementing changes in Portuguese tax legislation may not always consider the impact of the changes on the Madeira off-shore legislation. For example, a recent change in the law relating to dividend withholding tax resulted in questions about whether certain off-shore companies were still exempt from dividend withholding tax. The doubt was favorably resolved, but this type of difficulty may recur. The solution seems to be constant vigilance by the Madeira Trade Development Council (SDM) on behalf of the off-shore industry. One has to assume that, once a problem of this nature has been identified, the Lisbon authorities will be receptive to enactment of a correction. Nevertheless, as long as the regional government of Madeira is dependent on the good will of the central government, this risk will remain.

Tax treaties are currently in force between Portugal and a number of other countries as such they do not exclude Madeira off-shore companies.

Companies registered under the Madeira Free Trade Zone legislation can take advantage of these double-taxation treaties as regards receipt of funds into the company from investments into those other countries. They may make payments on loans without any withholding tax, having regard to the exemptions from all forms of Portuguese taxation provided by the free trade zone legislation.

Table 13.1 reflects the withholding tax rates applied to the residents of countries with tax treaties in force with Portugal.

There are no specific anti-avoidance restrictions that apply to companies operating under the Madeira Free Trade Zone legislation, as such companies are not liable to tax in Portugal.

Tax information exchange agreements are likely to be applied to the extent that assistance is sought for the reduction of tax as a result

Table 13.1. Withholding tax rates.

	Interest %	Dividends %	Royalties %
Austria	10	15	5/10
Belgium	15	15	5
Brazil	15	15	10/15
Denmark	15	10/15	10
Finland	15	10/15	5
Germany	10/15	15	10
Italy	15	15	12
Norway	15	10/15	10
Spain	15	10/15	5
Switzerland	10	10/15	5
United Kingdom	10	10/15	5

of any double-taxation agreements entered into between Portugal and other countries. Otherwise, the degree to which information can be required to be made available to the tax authorities remains to be clarified. Accounts must be filed, even though there is no obligation to make any tax payments.

Exchange control in Portugal is regulated by the Central Bank of Portugal. Companies established under the free trade zone legislation of Madeira are exempt from all exchange control regulations otherwise applicable in Portugal. There is no requirement for such companies to operate only in foreign currencies.

ADVANTAGES TO MADEIRA FREE TRADE ZONE COMPANIES

Industrial and Commercial Companies

A company engaged in almost any form of industrial or commercial activity within the Madeira Free Trade Zone will enjoy the following benefits:

■ "Total exemption from customs duties on imports into the zone;

- No quotas on exports to EEC countries, except those normally applicable to Portugal;

- Customs duties on imports into EEC countries based only on the value of raw materials and components that originate outside the EEC; no customs duties if all materials and components originate inside the ECC;

- Exemption from transfer tax and gift and inheritance tax on the acquisition of real estate for the purpose of setting up in the zone;

- Exemption from capital gains tax on the sale of fixed assets;

- Exemption from corporate income taxes on profits until December 31, 2011;

- Exemption from municipal property and other local taxes; and

- Exemption from withholding tax on interest on funds borrowed for investment in the zone and on royalty and know-how payments." (H.A. Sherman 1990.)

A company that invests in the capital of companies set up in the zone will be exempt from all withholding and income taxes on dividends and interest as well as share transfers.

A 50% subsidy for the cost of staff training and a grant of up to 50% of the cost of energy-saving changes in production methods together with the exemption of not deducting social security contributions from the wages of trainees or apprentices under the age of 22 are further incentives offered to industrial companies.

Tax Incentives for Investors

In addition to the general system of tax incentives applicable to investors operating in Portugal, entities investing in the capital of companies operating in the Madeira Free Trade Zone are entitled to:

- A 100% deduction for the capital invested from the profits of the investing entity liable to Portuguese corporate tax;

■ Complete exemption from withholding and income taxes on dividends, interest on shareholders' loans, and any other type of income received by the investors from these companies;

■ Exemption from capital gains tax on capital increases in these companies; and

■ Exemption from conveyance tax and gift and inheritance tax for all transfer of shares or other forms of participation in the capital of companies operating exclusively in the zone.

Banking

Regulation and supervision of all off-shore banking activities is conducted by the Madeira Development Company and the Portuguese Central Bank.

Financial institutions set up in Madeira are exempt from the corporation tax, capital gains tax, investment income tax, stamp duties, and value added tax. In addition, there are no exchange controls, and the institutions pay low initial and annual fees.

TAX-AVOIDANCE STRATEGIES

Financing a Company

Companies incorporated under the free trade zone legislation of Madeira are not subject to restrictions on the repatriation of funds, whether income or capital. No withholding taxes are retained in Madeira. There are no restrictions on payments of dividends from Madeira by free trade zone companies. Redeemable shares are permitted, and no taxes are levied on accumulated profits.

Companies incorporated under the free trade zone legislation need no permission to receive funds. As there is no tax, there are no concessions. Profits may be accumulated free of tax. Free trade zone companies are also exempted from the exchange control regulations generally applicable in Portugal. There are no restrictions on the issue or redemption of shares, except to ensure that the company meets the minimum share capital required under Portuguese company law and legal reserve obligations. Free trade zone companies may take advantage of Portugal's double-taxation agreements.

Holding Companies

A holding company can be established under the free trade zone legislation of Madeira that will be exempt from general taxes in Portugal. There appears to be an advantage in organizing holding companies in Madeira to retain the interest in companies incorporated and operated in those countries with which Portugal has a double-taxation treaty.

Finance Companies

There are no banking or exchange controls in Madeira that apply to enterprises established under the Madeira Free Trade Zone legislation. Funds may be freely transmitted or repatriated in any convertible currency. Accounts in Madeira in currencies other than Portuguese Escudos must be maintained with banks licensed to operate under the free trade zone legislation. However, companies are permitted to maintain accounts and balances with financial institutions elsewhere in the world. There are no withholding taxes or other taxes on income or capital, and funds may be remitted or repatriated free of any tax where the enterprise is authorized under the free trade zone legislation. There does seem to be an advantage in licensing from Madeira rights to companies operating in countries that have a double-taxation agreement with Portugal.

Trading Companies

No special regulations or taxes apply to trading companies operating under the free trade zone legislation of Madeira.

Advantages can be obtained by securing trading through a company incorporated in Portugal under the Madeira Free Trade Zone legislation. Companies whose activities are of an industrial or commercial nature (in particular, manufacturing, assembling, packing, or merely warehousing of goods) can be offered particular advantages in Madeira, provided that these activities or the goods produced or handled do not present any threat to national security, public health, or the natural environment.

In particular, these companies may receive total exemption from customs duties on goods or raw materials imported into the Madeira Free Trade Zone and exemption from quotas on the export to EEC countries of goods produced in the zone other than those exemptions not normally provided to Portugal. This exemption is likely to be a major attraction for manufacturers, especially non-EEC manufacturers.

In addition, goods produced in the free trade zone and imported into the EEC are subject to customs duty only on the value of the imported raw materials and components originating from outside the EEC.

There are also likely to be further advantages available to companies operating and trading through Madeira within the EEC after the easing of tariff barriers after 1992.

Shipping Companies

Under the free trade zone legislation, an opportunity now exists to establish shipping companies in Madeira. A separate international ships registry has been created in Madeira to provide for the registration of vessels owned by Portuguese companies. The vessels themselves are registered as operating under the Portuguese flag.

Where the vessels are owned by a company licensed under the free trade zone legislation, the activities of the vessel outside Portugal are not subject to tax.

TAX CONSIDERATIONS FOR THE U.S. INVESTOR

As discussed earlier, Madeira's unique relationship with Portugal allows potential U.S. exporters into Europe to assemble the last percentages of their product in the tax-free trade zone. In addition, through Madeira's agreements with Portugal, U.S. companies incur extremely low customs or import duties. Thus, a U.S. exporter can set up a manufacturing plant in Madeira's free-trade zone and take advantage of most of the European Community's benefits. (See also Chapter 15, The 1992 Factor.)

14

Bahamas

The off-shore business in the Bahamas has recently undergone a renaissance that will dramatically enhance the stature of the islands as an international financial center. The leading edge of this renaissance is a new program of legislation which comprises the International Business Companies (IBC) Act and the Creation of Trusts Act. The main beneficiary for the Bahamas' new legislation has been the International Business Companies Act. This statute, more than any other, has contributed to the renewal of interest in the Bahamas, in that it provides a dramatic concessionary and liberal regime for the incorporation and management of off-shore companies.

An IBC is a company that does not carry on business with persons resident in the Bahamas, nor owns any interest in real or leasehold property situated in the Bahamas, except in the form of leased premises for use as an office. An IBC cannot carry on banking and/or trust business, although it may act as a trustee of a private family trust if that is its sole purpose. An IBC may also not act as an insurer. It is worth noting that inspection of the books and records of an IBC is limited to a shareholder, thereby ensuring the confidentiality of the identity of the owners of an IBC.

The many advantages offered by the IBC Act include:

- The IBC Act exempts transfers of property and transactions in respect of the shares from the stamp tax for 20 years from the date of incorporation.

- Nominative or bearer shares at owner's option.

- Exchange Control Regulations do not apply to IBCs nor to any transactions between shareholders of an IBC in respect of shares in an IBC.

- IBCs and shareholders of IBCs are not subject to any business license fee, income tax, corporation tax, capital gains tax, or any other tax on income or distributions accruing to or derived from the IBC or any other transaction to which the IBC or its shareholders may be a party.

- An IBC has virtually unlimited powers and judicial capacity granted an individual.

- Companies already incorporated in the Bahamas, as well as companies incorporated outside the Bahamas, are permitted to register under the new Act and through this "transplanted registration"—to continue their corporate existence as fully fledged IBCs.

- Companies incorporated in other jurisdictions are able to provisionally register under the IBC Act in order to hedge against the uncertainty of the company's present jurisdiction. If and when the need arises to "export" such a company to the Bahamas, all that need be done is to serve the requisite notice, and the registration becomes complete.

- Incorporation fees, licensing fees, and annual fees have been dramatically lowered, thereby giving the Bahamas a competitive advantage in terms of cost. Fees for incorporation range from $100 to $1000 depending on the authorized capital.

This legislation has been in existence just over a year and the success of it is evidenced by the number of incorporations exceeding 4500 in the same period of time. This exceptional growth has been facilitated by the availability of a 24-hour incorporation process.

POLITICAL STABILITY

The Bahamas has a long record of political, social, and economic stability and the business climate is excellent, with no taxes on income, profits, or capital gains. The Bahamas' close proximity to the United States (same time zone with New York, Miami, and Toronto) has created the following advantages: most Bahamian goods enjoy duty and quota free entry into the U.S. under the Caribbean Basin Initiative. The Bahamian dollar is maintained at parity with the U.S. dollar, ensuring exchange rate stability with the U.S. market.

For foreign investors the government offers a wide range of incentives, including exemption from import duties, tax holidays, low cost land and factory space, and free-trade zone facilities. The Bahamas also permits the unrestricted repatriation of dividends, profits, and capital.

PROSPECTS

With such momentous events on the horizon as the unification of Europe in 1992 and the reversion of Hong Kong to China in 1997, the world financial community faces a very uncertain future. Operational benefits from utilizing the Bahamas can be found in the low cost of raising funds in the Euromarket without having to pay the attendant charges in the United States in the form of minimum reserve requirements, thus effectively lowering the cost of funding for the bank. Furthermore, the European Community has established benefits with the Bahamas and other Caribbean and African countries that enable intermediary companies located in the Bahamas (such as U.S. exporters) to dramatically reduce import and customs duties as well as license fees when entering the European market. Thus, the Bahamas offers attractive conditions for a U.S. exporter to assemble the last 20 to 30 percent of his product in the jurisdiction and then re-export the completed product to Europe. For foreign investors in the United States—such as Lloyds Bank of London, which has recently set up its Americas headquarters in Nassau—the favorable investment climate, the freedom from regulatory controls, the excellent telecommunications system, the proximity to major cities, the number of skilled professionals in the industry and the extremely low tax base and limited controls create an environment not offered in many places in the region. As a result of the Caribbean Basin Initiative foreigners who wish to reach the American markets are able to achieve lower taxes and import duties and duty-free exemptions for certain goods. In 1991, the Bahamas passed the Fraudulent Dispositions Act, which enables Bahamian trusts to be established with certainty—especially in regard to how thwarted creditors can legally challenge the Bahamian Asset Protection Trust. The Act clearly invalidates a trust that is set up to defraud. The Asset Protection Trust was launched for the legitimate protection of assets and is designed not to protect a person against contingent creditors of which he might be aware, but from future illegitimate claimants.

The recent expiration of tax treaties between the United States and Bermuda and Barbados should assist the Bahamian captive business. The alarming fluctuations in insurance prices are creating budgeting problems for many corporations. By forming a captive, this allows the parent company to stabilize (and control) its insurance costs.

15

The 1992 Factor

The scheduled unification of the European Economic Community in 1992 contains two elements relevant to a discussion of tax haven centers: the creation of a single barrier-free market among the twelve member states and the harmonization of their systems of taxation.

A unified European market offers many opportunities for businesses that position themselves to take advantage of its benefits. "Fortress Europe," the term frequently used to describe the unified market, is most untrue from the perspective of U.S. businesses. The opportunity of reaching a market of over 400 million people employing some of the strongest currencies in the world in relation to the U.S. Dollar, particularly the British Pound and the German Mark, should not be overlooked or underestimated. The countries most threatened by "Fortress Europe" are Australia and Japan, which might find it increasingly difficult to penetrate the relevant tariff walls.

It is clear that those companies and individuals from outside Europe who have already established manufacturing or other bases in Europe prior to 1992, and thus are inside the tariff walls, will be in a more certain position, whatever the eventual outcome of import and external customs duties. Any special arrangements made between businesses and European governments before 1992 will be honored thereafter regardless of EEC regulations in force for the unified market. With this in mind, the Irish authorities have introduced a number of incentive schemes to encourage non-Europeans to manufacture in Ireland and qualify for the benefits of Ireland's tax treaties. In a typical application of this procedure, a U.S. business may manufacture the components of a product in California that is intended for eventual consumption in Europe. If it then ships the components to Ireland for final assembly, the product will receive an Irish certificate of origin and be eligible for barrier-free trade in Europe. As an additional incentive, 75% of turnover of a product so manufactured will qualify for tax of only 10%. Moreover, by extracting service and management fees from the Irish operation to the United States, most U.S. exporters will drastically reduce their tax obligations. These incentives will remain valid until the year 2005 and most likely beyond.

For the U.S. corporation, tax havens or low tax jurisdictions are of prime benefit where the U.S. corporation suffers greater than 34 percent tax on its foreign operations. By effectively using jurisdictions that tax at rates lower then the United States (i.e., 34 percent) the corporation is able to reduce its excess foreign tax credit position.

As for the new Europe, there is a need for specialized services for the would-be U.S. exporter, covering the emerging body of common European law, in particular the rapidly expanding body of regulations propounded by the European bureaucracy in Brussels. It is no longer enough for an exporter to maintain an office in London. On-the-spot representation in Brussels is already important and will become indispensable after 1992.

It is clear that the unification of European markets will result in a shake-out of non-European exporters. Whether already in existence or created through mergers or take-overs, giant firms able to take advantage of economies of scale will thrive. So will small, specialized firms aiming at niche markets. Medium-sized firms lacking either economies of scale or specialized products will suffer. To this extent, the new Europe will resemble the present United States.

Lessons for non-Europeans intending to export to Europe are clear: aim for the niche products for which a market will always be open and establish alliances with firms within the community walls to take advantage of local marketing skills. As in the case of Ireland, tariff and non-tariff barriers can be circumvented by manufacturing in other European areas offering incentives, such as Madeira and Toulon.

The harmonization of the tax systems of the EEC member states has already encountered severe obstacles. Dutch and Luxembourg authorities have been steadfastly reluctant to impose withholding taxes, for example, and it is generally accepted that structures of direct taxation will not be harmonized. For the time being, agreement appears possible only on indirect taxation, such as the value added tax, but it is not likely that the European Community will be able to harmonize the entire European tax base. As such tremendous opportunities will exist for nonresident individuals and corporations owning businesses in foreign countries to use intermediary companies and structures so as to benefit from a third country's low tax rate and low cost of financing. A clear sign of tax haven benefits with the fast-approaching unification process has been the extraordinary growth of Gibraltar (12 percent GNP growth over the last two years), Madeira, and Luxembourg.

After many years of frustrated efforts, the EC seems finally to have reached agreement on a cross-border corporate tax regime that will meet the objectives of the single market by not harmonizing corporate tax rates, systems and withholding taxes but rather to establish a package of proposals designed to eliminate tax penalties on businesses operating across several member states of the community.

The prospect of tax harmonization in Europe was not at all attractive to the Channel Islands, which over the years had achieved considerable economic prosperity. Inevitably, it seemed that the harmonization directives would be extended to the Islands. Alternatively, the Islands could have been excluded altogether from the Community, which would have meant that they would be excluded from the only feasible market for their horticultural and agricultural produce and would have threatened their popularity as a tax haven. However, after long negotiations among the European Economic Community, the U.K. government, and the Islands, agreement was reached on an amendment to the Treaty of Rome and a protocol to the Treaty of Accession. Essentially, these exclude the Islands from all aspects of the Treaty of Rome other than those relating to free trade in agricultural and industrial products.

Therefore, the Islands have now achieved a special status in relation to EEC countries, and there are many different situations in which considerable potential advantages may be obtained. However, this privileged position depends to a considerable extent upon the high degree of internal supervision that both Guernsey and Jersey maintain. The manner in which the Island authorities monitor financial activities is fundamental to the preservation of Guernsey and Jersey as highly respectable and reliable financial centers. Consequently, the Island authorities will not countenance either residents or outsiders using their territories for evasive activity.

When dealing with Jersey, Guernsey, and the Isle of Man, it is important to remember that all three are associate members of the European Economic Community. They retain independence and are not bound to comply with Community financial, commercial, or economic policies, except in respect of the common external tariff and the Community system of agricultural levies and border control.

Madeira, the European Community's newest international business center, is an autonomous region with a rapidly developing free trade zone, off-shore financial center, and shipping register. With its many tax incentives for financial institutions and other tax advantages available through the operation of Portuguese double-taxation treaties, Madeira is poised to become one of the European Community's most exciting centers.

It is interesting to note that the off-shore industry in the Caribbean Islands remains optimistic that the need for its services will not diminish. With 1992 looming for Europe, posing a potential threat to some European tax havens, and with the 1997 transfer of Hong Kong to China following soon after, some believe the prospects for growth for the Caribbean centers may be better than ever.

With the growth of the European market over the last decade and the effects of 1992, corporations are establishing themselves in Europe through not only cross-border mergers and acquisitions, but through joint ventures (Phillip Morris/Jacob Suchard and Guinness/LVMH) and the accumulation of foreign businesses (Ford/Jaguar), which are only partly digested and remain semi-independent units, coordinated by lean financial headquarters in Europe.

In contrast, the traditional multinational firm transplanted management and grew mainly through direct investment in foreign plant, equipment, and buildings, often in the process destroying the national identities of acquisition targets. Mergers and acquisitions accounted for 56 percent of total foreign direct investment of U.S., U.K., German, and Japanese firms in 1989; traditional multinational growth contributed 44 percent. This compares to only 25.7 percent for mergers and acquisitions in 1984 and 74.3 percent for traditional multinational growth.

The approach of 1992 will bring into play the global importance of utilizing tax havens or low tax jurisdictions so as to facilitate global expansion while monitoring both operating and tax costs.

The single European market may encourage multinationals to consider flotations of their European businesses on one (or more) European exchanges. In addition, the capital demands of Eastern Europe may need to be met from European markets, given the capital shortages that are appearing worldwide.

As an example, a U.S. multinational seeking to expand its existing Western European operations into the East may need to depend upon European equity capital. In fact because Europe will become an important equity investment center the opportunity of low cost financing in a tax haven will have more broad-based appeal. Already, foreign companies (i.e. U.S., Australia. . .) are chasing these pools of global money by choosing to list their shares on international stock exchanges. Particularly attractive at present is the Luxembourg holding company and co-ordination company as well as low-tax Belgium co-ordination centers, Madeira and Gibraltar export and exempt companies and Irish nonresident corporations. These company structures all offer reduced tax and operating costs such as import/export and customs duties.

For an American exporter wanting to break into the European market, various tax haven jurisdictions offer perfect solutions to reduce tax and operating costs for the exporter.

Figure 15.1. U.S. Exporter's use of foreign manufacturer.

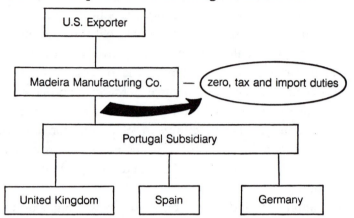

For example, it is possible for a U.S. exporter to manufacture the major proportion of his product in the United States and then establish a processing plant in Madeira which will assemble the final parts of the product. By utilizing the processing plant, the U.S. exporter is able to operate from a free-trade zone and through Madeira's relationship with Portugal, the exporter is able to enter the European market with dramatically lower customs and import duties as a direct result of Portugal's member status in the EEC. The U.S. exporter will further benefit from low withholding tax treatments between its Portuguese and Madeira companies and the other European subsidiaries/branches that it controls (see Figure 15.1).

The impact of U.S. corporations entering Europe by establishing subsidiary operations, will force proper planning to be done in order to receive withholding taxes between the different European countries. For example, if the U.S. corporation has its European headquarters in London it may be possible for the U.S. parent to reduce its withholding taxes by establishing a Netherlands subsidiary—in the case of royalties from Spain to the United Kingdom, these attract a 10 percent withholding tax, while if repatriated through the Netherlands zero tax will be suffered—similarly with dividends from Italy, Spain, and Finland. In the case of interest payments, using a Spanish or Irish company to own the Italian operation and would reduce the withholding tax on Italian interest payments to 12 and 10 percent, respectively; as against utilizing the U.K. recipient company which would suffer 15 percent withholding tax. (Table 15.1 shows European withholding taxes on dividends, interest, and royalties.)

PART THREE

Concerns for U.S. Taxpayers

16

Foreign Tax Credits

The foreign tax credit is the principal mechanism provided by the U.S. Internal Revenue Code for eliminating international double taxation of corporate taxpayers. U.S. companies are entitled to a direct dollar-for-dollar reduction in their U.S. tax liabilities for foreign income taxes imposed on foreign-source income earned directly or through subsidiaries. However, the maximum allowable credit is limited to the U.S. taxes otherwise payable in respect of the company's foreign-source taxable income as calculated according to U.S. tax-accounting principles. The maximum allowable foreign tax credit is thus generally equal to foreign-source taxable income multiplied by the U.S. corporate tax rate.

Foreign tax credits greater than the maximum allowable credit are excess foreign tax credits. Excess foreign tax credits can be carried back two years, then forward five years in search of foreign-source taxable income. Any excess foreign tax credits not used during these eight years will be lost.

The Tax Reform Act of 1986 included four major changes relevant to the taxation of foreign-source income and the availability of foreign tax credits.

First, the 1986 Act expanded the circumstances in which income earned by a foreign subsidiary will be currently taxed to its U.S. parent, even though the income is not distributed as a dividend. At the same time, the Act made effective credit utilization more difficult by requiring that the foreign tax credit limitation be calculated separately for different "baskets" of income. These baskets include passive income, high withholding tax interest income, financial services income, shipping income, dividends from each non-U.S.-controlled foreign subsidiary, and a residual basket for foreign income not included in any other basket. This change reduced the ability of U.S. corporations to combine high-tax and low-tax foreign income to "average down" high foreign taxes. Third, the act set forth new rules for the allocation of a pro rata share of U.S. interest and general administrative expenses against foreign income, which can sharply reduce the maximum allowable credit. Finally, the Act reduced the U.S. corporate income tax rate from 46% to 34%, which in and of itself created "excess" or unusable credits for many U.S. companies.

CALCULATING THE MAXIMUM FOREIGN TAX CREDIT

The foreign tax credit allowed against the U.S. tax on worldwide income in a given tax year is the lesser of:

■ The foreign tax actually or deemed paid or

■ The U.S. tax rate applied to the portion of worldwide taxable income considered to be foreign-source taxable income under U.S. law. This limitation may be expressed as:

$$\text{U.S. Tax on Worldwide Taxable Income} \times \frac{\text{Foreign-Source Taxable Income}}{\text{Worldwide Taxable Income}}$$

An example of the way this calculation is employed is the case of Multinational A, which has $100 million of worldwide taxable income, including $30 million of foreign-source taxable income, and which paid $15 million in foreign income taxes. If the U.S. tax rate is 34%, the foreign tax credit limitation calculated on the U.S. rate is:

$$\$34 \text{ million} \times \frac{\$30 \text{ million}}{\$100 \text{ million}} = \$10.2 \text{ million}$$

Since the foreign tax credit calculated on the U.S. tax rate is less than the foreign tax actually paid, $10.2 million is the maximum credit allowed. This will result in an excess foreign tax credit of $4.8 million, the difference between $15 million and $10.2 million.

Whenever a U.S. corporation does business in at least one foreign country with a tax rate higher than the U.S. rate, it will be faced with the prospect of an excess foreign tax credit.

Excess Foreign Tax Credits

U.S. taxpayers with foreign operations find themselves with excess foreign tax credits for one or more of the following reasons:

- The decline in the top U.S. corporate tax rate from 46% in the early 1980s to 40% in 1987 and 34% thereafter. The lower the U.S. tax rate, the more likely it becomes that foreign operations will be taxed locally at a rate higher than the U.S. rate.

- Foreign-source income must be divided in up to nine "baskets," each subject to its own tax-credit limitation. This takes away the ability to average out tax rates paid, because "active," highly taxed income is more likely to be in a separate basket than lower taxed "passive" income.

- The rules for interest-expense allocation have been made more strict.

Impact of Lower U.S. Rates

It is true, of course, that lower U.S. tax rates may reduce the total taxes paid by many U.S. multinational corporations. At the same time, limited foreign operations will cause excess foreign tax credits.

Consider the case of Global, Inc. Its $10 million of annual taxable income consists of one-half U.S. and one-half foreign-source income. The foreign tax rate remains constant at 46%. When the U.S. tax rate was 46% as well, no excess foreign tax credit resulted, and one-half of total taxes was payable to the United States. In other words, Global paid foreign taxes at a rate of 46% on $5 million, or $2.3 million. Before allowance for the foreign tax credit, its U.S. tax on worldwide income was 46% of $10 million, or $4.6 million. The foreign tax credit limitation was

$$\$4.6 \text{ million} \times \frac{\$5 \text{ million}}{\$10 \text{ million}}$$

or $2.3 million. U.S. tax due after deducting the credit was $2.3 million, there was no excess foreign tax credit, and the total tax due, foreign and domestic, was $4.6 million.

When the U.S. tax rate dropped to 40%, the U.S. tax on world-wide income was $4 million and the foreign tax credit was $2 million. U.S. tax due after deducting the credit was $2 million, there was an excess foreign tax credit of $300,000, and the total tax due to foreign and domestic authorities was $4.3 million.

When the U.S. rate dropped to 34%, the U.S. tax on worldwide income was $3.4 million and the foreign tax credit was $1.7 million. U.S. tax due after deducting the credit was $1.7 million, there was an excess foreign tax credit of $600,000, and the total tax due to both authorities was $4 million.

However, as foreign-source taxable income becomes a higher per-centage of worldwide taxable income, the total taxes payable world-wide become less and less affected by the U.S. rate. In the extreme case, where all taxable income is from foreign sources, the only im-pact of a reduced U.S. tax rate is an excess foreign tax credit to be carried back two years and forward five.

Table 16.1 shows the impact of a U.S. tax rate below the foreign tax rate as taxable income from foreign sources becomes an increasing percentage of a given $10 million of worldwide income. The foreign tax rate is assumed to be 50% and the U.S. rate is 34%.

Table 16.1. Effect on excess foreign tax credit of increased foreign-source income ($millions).

Worldwide Taxable Income	Foreign Source Taxable Income	U.S. Source Taxable Income	Foreign Tax Payable	U.S. Tax Prior to Credit	Foreign Tax Credit	U.S. Tax Payable	Total Tax Payable	Excess Foreign Tax Credit
$10	$2	$8	$1	$3.4	$.68	$2.72	$3.72	$.32
10	4	6	2	3.4	1.36	2.04	4.04	.64
10	6	4	3	3.4	2.04	1.36	4.36	.96
10	8	2	4	3.4	2.72	.68	4.68	1.28
10	10	0	5	3.4	3.40	0	5.00	1.60

Interest-Expense Allocations

U.S. multinational corporations prefer to characterize as much income as possible as foreign-source income to increase their foreign tax credit.

Before the Tax Reform Act of 1986, interest expense was allocated on a U.S. company-by-company basis. As a result, if a U.S. corporation borrowed funds, all interest was considered a U.S. expense.

To foil the strategy of "U.S. borrowing" to finance intercompany loans to foreign subsidiaries, the Internal Revenue Code now requires that the interest expense on loans by U.S.-affiliated companies be consolidated and allocated between U.S.-source and foreign-source income in proportion to the ratio of foreign assets to worldwide assets. This allocation is expressed in the following formula:

$$\text{Interest Expense to Reduce Foreign-Source Income} = \text{Total Interest Expense} \times \frac{\text{Foreign Assets}}{\text{Worldwide Assets}}$$

This allocation must be made without regard for where the funds were actually raised, even if all funds were borrowed in the United States. This allocation reduces the foreign tax credit by reducing foreign-source taxable income for U.S. purposes without reducing foreign taxes paid.

Consider again the case of Multinational A, which has worldwide taxable income of $100 million, foreign-source taxable income of $30 million, worldwide assets of $300 million, and foreign assets of $100 million. If Multinational A borrows $60 million at an annual interest rate of 10% and was previously unleveraged, its total annual interest expense will be $6 million. The amount of interest expense that must be allocated to reduce foreign-source taxable income will be

$$\$6 \text{ million} \times \frac{\$100 \text{ million}}{\$300 \text{ million}}$$

or $2 million. Foreign-source taxable income will therefore be reduced from $30 million to $28 million. Worldwide taxable income will be reduced by the interest expense from $100 million to $94 million, and the foreign tax credit at a U.S. rate of 34% will be

$$\$34 \text{ million} \times \frac{\$28 \text{ million}}{\$94 \text{ million}}$$

or $10.1 million. Thus, as a result of allocating the interest expense, Multinational A's foreign tax credit has been reduced from $10.2 million to $10.1 million, a loss of $100,000.

Ford Motor Co. recently came up with a way to preserve its foreign-tax credits and avoid paying a tax penalty, after acquiring a highly leveraged consumer and commercial finance company that would have had the effect of dramatically increasing foreign interest expense allocations. The solution was to form Ford Holdings, a new umbrella entity for its leasing and insurance units just prior to the acquisition of the new finance company. The key to overcoming the consolidation rule lies in Ford Holdings' ownership structure. Ford the parent bought back all the common stock in Holdings and then issued preferred stock with voting rights equivalent to 25% of the voting power and value of Holdings. By selling more than 20% to third-party shareholders, Ford effectively deconsolidated Ford Holdings and qualified it to be considered a separate group for tax purposes. The requirement that Ford own less than 80% of the vote and value of Holdings is an ongoing test that must be met every single day in the forseeable future. If there is any one day in which Ford's control exceeds 80%, then Holdings fails the test, the group must be consolidated with Ford again, and the company will then have to wait 5 years for the opportunity to become deconsolidated once more. This structure is expected to save the company $1 billion in U.S. taxes by preserving the status quo with its foreign-tax credits.

REDUCING EXCESS FOREIGN TAX CREDITS

A company can reduce its excess foreign tax credits in three general ways:

- By reducing foreign taxes directly, for example, by taking advantage of tax holidays or investing in tax shelters in countries with high income taxes;
- By increasing foreign-source taxable income as defined by U.S. tax law without necessarily affecting any foreign tax liability; examples include using non-recourse financing of domestic property to avoid interest-expense allocations to foreign-source taxable income and choosing the local currency as the functional currency;
- By combining the above, for example, by direct third-party financing in a high-tax country; in that case, not only are foreign taxes reduced but the interest is excluded from reallocation.

Reducing Foreign Taxes

Foreign taxes can be reduced through treaty shopping, transfer pricing, leasing and other tax shelters, and tax holidays abroad.

Treaty Shopping. A corporation may establish operations abroad solely to benefit from tax treaties that will reduce foreign taxes. This practice, known as "treaty shopping," is discouraged by the Internal Revenue Service and the U.S. Treasury Department. The U.S. government has recently renegotiated tax treaties with the British Virgin Islands and the Netherlands Antilles in response to "excessive use" of treaty shopping in those jurisdictions.

Treaty-shopping opportunities still exist in many European countries, however. For example, Corporation A receives $1 million a year in royalties from Australian patents. Australia taxes royalties received by a U.S. corporation at the regular rate of 46% of net income, resulting in an Australian tax liability of $460,000. By the simple expedient of sublicensing the patents to a Netherlands subsidiary for $900,000 (providing a 10% profit to the subsidiary), Corporation A can receive the benefits of the Netherlands tax treaties and reduce its foreign tax liability dramatically. The tax savings under this arrangement are outlined in Table 16.2.

Table 16.2. Tax reduction through treaty shopping.

Australian 10% withholding tax on $1 million of royalties paid to Netherlands	$100,000
Netherlands 50% tax on corporate profits	50,000
Netherlands tax on $900,000 of royalties to the U.S. parent	(none)
Netherlands 5% withholding tax on dividend paid to U.S. parent	2,500
Total foreign tax liability	$152,500

As a result of treaty shopping, Corporation A has reduced the effective foreign tax rate from 46% to 15.25%.

Transfer pricing. One way to reduce foreign taxes directly is through transfer pricing. By this method, when a U.S. firm is exporting to a subsidiary, if it charges a higher price for the export, it will earn more profits in the United States and a lower profit abroad.

Internal Revenue Code §482 and its accompanying regulations contain detailed rules allowing the IRS to recompute transfer prices and reallocate profits if the transfer price is not "fair" and not at "arm's length." Most countries also have rules on determining the "correct" transfer price, but these rules are generally not as distinctly defined.

If a taxpayer must adjust its U.S. transfer price for tax purposes, the result is one price for U.S. and another for foreign purposes, causing double taxation. Although all U.S. foreign tax treaties contain procedures for avoiding double taxation, they may be both expensive and cumbersome to enforce. However, a U.S. multinational firm with a high excess foreign tax credit has little or nothing to lose. A prime reason for the low tax paid by Japanese manufacturers in the United States is the incredible mark-up on cost that their U.S. subsidiaries must pay thereby reducing the subsidiaries margins considerably.

Tax shelters. Investing in tax shelters abroad can generate tax losses to offset taxable income in selected countries, thus reducing foreign taxes directly. Foreign leveraged leasing involving depreciable property is ideal for this purpose. For example, the foreign subsidiary of a large U.S. multinational company may reduce its foreign taxes by becoming an equity participant in property leases. The depreciation tax shields that result from ownership will tend to reduce the tax expense of the subsidiary.

If possible, the leasing activity should take place in countries with high tax rates, such as Germany or Australia, and the subsidiary should have ample funds available for this purpose. As a practical matter, however, the largest U.S. multinationals are unlikely to undertake tax-sheltered investments abroad.

Tax holidays. Foreign countries sometimes offer a tax holiday, that is, a period of time during which income from a new business may be received free of tax. Although limitations are sometimes imposed, this practice induces companies to locate in tax-holiday countries.

In the past, U.S. companies often neglected to take advantage of such incentives because the final result was not changed: the company had to pay the U.S. tax, but could not take a credit for foreign taxes paid.

Today, tax holidays should be viewed with more interest. If a company has excess foreign tax credit, a tax holiday may make the foreign income effectively tax-free.

Increasing Foreign-Source Taxable Income

Several strategies are available to increase foreign-source taxable income.

Global Dividend Policy—The Dividend Remittance Program.
To use foreign tax credits effectively, many multinationals have
attempted to design a dividend policy that produces the lowest
overall foreign taxable income. With a U.S. tax rate of only 34%
as a cap on the foreign tax credit, it is possible that no combination of foreign dividends may produce a lower average tax on foreign-source income than the U.S. rate. In such cases, foreign
dividend policy is likely to be more tax neutral than in the past.

However, as a tool to reduce excess foreign tax credits, the
dividend remittance program, a strategy popular in the past, still
may be of some use. The level and frequency of dividends paid to
a U.S. parent by its foreign subsidiaries typically are a result of
negotiations between the finance and tax departments that take
into account both financial needs and the tax consequences of
the policy. If the enterprise is in a "short" tax-credit situation,
dividends can be paid from a high-tax country. Conversely, when
a corporation has excess tax credits, which currently is more
likely, dividend payments from low-tax countries can be stepped
up as much as possible. In this way, the numerator in the foreign
tax credit limitation formula is increased relatively more than foreign taxes paid, assuming that the foreign tax rate is lower than
the U.S. rate.

Changes in Corporate Structure and Transaction Locations. In
many cases, a corporation may change its form and the place of its
corporate presence or transactions with relative ease. Techniques that
minimize excess foreign tax credits include the following:

■ Title to property sold to foreign customers should change
abroad to increase foreign-source taxable income for U.S.
purposes. For example, property should be sold F.O.B. destination, rather than F.A.S. (Free Alongside Ship). Under
the Tax Reform Act of 1986, sales of personal property are
deemed to take place in the country of the seller. However,
this new rule does not cover sales in the ordinary course of
business.

■ Some transactions should be channeled through subsidiaries set up in intermediary countries to the extent necessary to take advantage of tax treaties or special tax incentives.

■ To take advantage of low U.S. tax rates, some foreign operations might be relocated to the United States.

Deduction-Allocation Strategies.   The typical multinational corporation has operations in several countries taxed at a rate higher than the U.S. tax rate of 34%, as well as foreign-source passive income taxed at lower rates in a separate basket. U.S. tax regulations contain guidelines and options for allocating general expenses among sources of income.

A taxpayer should follow two principles when allocating expenses:

1. Where possible, deductions should be allocated to U.S. income. This increases foreign-source taxable income, which increases the foreign tax credit available. One example is the use of self-liquidating domestic non-recourse loans to avoid interest-expense allocation altogether.

2. Where a firm must allocate the expense to foreign-source income, it should allocate it to the lowest tax basket, which yields the lowest contribution to the overall foreign tax credit in any event. An example is the allocation of investment expenses against passive income subject to low rates of withholding abroad.

Passive-to-Active Income Reclassification.   Passive income, such as royalties, generally is subject to a lower tax rate abroad than is active income, such as income from sales and services. Because passive income goes into a separate basket for foreign tax credit limitation purposes, the foreign tax credit frequently is reduced.

There are four strategies that transfer passive income to the active income basket:

1. In some cases, foreign subsidiaries that have a license to use property and that pay royalties to the U.S. parent may purchase the property outright.

2. It is possible to change a royalty agreement to a service contract.

3. Passive income that a corporation transfers to a controlled foreign corporation is considered active if all passive income of the CFC is less than 5% of its total income.

4. Several countries tax administrative offices under special rules. For example, the tax may be computed under a cost-plus system with the tax base fixed at 10% of cost. Such a foreign service office could be established to facilitate the conversion of royalties to service income to reap the benefits of the treaty network.

Consider, for example, Company X, which has many activities abroad. Its passive basket is subject to a 15% tax abroad and its active basket to 40%. If the company moves $1 million from the passive basket to a $4 million active basket and the U.S. rate is 34%, the result is as follows:

1. The average tax rate in the active basket is reduced from 40% to [$4 × .40 + $1 × .15]/$5 × 100% or 35%. This is still above the U.S. tax rate but leaves Company X with a smaller excess foreign tax credit with respect to the active basket.

2. The tax credit available with respect to the $1 million of transformed passive income is now 34% (the lesser of 35% or 34%) rather than 15% (the lesser of 15% or 34%). Thus, the foreign tax credit for the year has increased by $190,000 (34% less 15% of $1 million).

Electing the Functional Currency. The Tax Reform Act of 1986 allows a taxpayer with foreign operations to elect the "functional currency," either the U.S. dollar or the applicable local currency. A taxpayer finding itself with excess foreign tax credit may well consider electing the local currency as its functional currency. This will cause a present increase in reported foreign earnings, resulting in a reduction of excess foreign tax credits coupled with decreased earnings later on. As a result, excess tax credits are less likely to expire.

The selection of both the countries and the companies for which this election is made should be considered carefully because the election is irrevocable. The election is available for a "Qualified Business Unit," which is defined as a separate trade or business that maintains separate books and records.

Increasing the Earnings of a Foreign Corporation by Election. U.S. tax regulations allow a U.S. shareholder in a foreign corporation to make tax elections affecting the computation of the foreign corporation's earnings, not the foreign tax payable. A few years ago, these elections were used primarily to reduce net income, thereby increasing the effective tax rate on foreign-source income for U.S. purposes. Currently, the opposite is true. Thus, a U.S. multinational corporation in a chronic excess foreign tax credit position might make whatever elections are available in the individual circumstances that would increase foreign earnings. Because this strategy defers U.S. tax benefits by increasing worldwide income taxed in the U.S., it should be used only as a last resort to preserve tax credits that otherwise most likely will be lost. Elections, once made, are irrevocable.

Non-recourse Financing of U.S. Property. If a corporation meets four requirements, interest on non-recourse loans secured by domestic property is excluded from the allocation between U.S.-source and foreign-source assets. The maximum use of such loans will increase foreign-source taxable income, thereby increasing the foreign tax credit limitation. The four requirements are:

1. The loan must be incurred exclusively and the proceeds actually used to acquire or improve specific domestic property.

2. The loan must be without recourse to the borrower and the rest of the borrower's assets. That is, the creditor must rely solely on the specific property as security for payment of prin-

cipal and interest on the loan. The creditor cannot look to any other property of the borrower or third party for payment on the loan.

3. The income from the financed property likely will be sufficient to pay off principal and interest.

4. The loan agreement must restrict the disposal of the financed property during the time the loan is outstanding.

The interest deduction will not be deemed wholly domestic if the motive for structuring the transaction in this way lacks economic substance. For example, a loan between a parent and a subsidiary would be deemed to have no economic substance.

Non-recourse financings might include mortgages on income-producing buildings or other property and project financings.

Additional Strategies

Exploiting Differences Between U.S. and Foreign Law.   A difficult but potentially rewarding strategy is to explore legal differences between U.S. and foreign definitions of financial instruments or institutions. This strategy might result in different tax treatment under each system. For example:

1. Foreign debt but U.S. equity. In some countries it may be possible to issue a security that would be treated as a debt instrument in the foreign country but as preferred stock in the United States. The "interest" paid would reduce foreign taxes directly. At the same time, for U.S. purposes, the foreign tax credit on "dividends" deemed paid would still be available.

2. Foreign corporation but U.S. branch. In some countries it might be possible to establish an entity regarded there as a corporation but treated as a branch under U.S. law. This would accelerate U.S. income without imposing foreign dividend withholding taxes. This strategy is most effective in

low-tax countries, including countries with an effective low-tax rate.

3. United States controlled corporation, but also, according to U.K. law the corporation is resident in the United Kingdom. Certain deductions may be taken in both countries as a resulting of the differing laws.

Foreign Third-Party Financing.   The easiest way to reduce the impact of the interest-allocation rules is to replace the scheme of U.S. borrowings followed by intercompany loans with third-party borrowing by foreign subsidiaries. This should be done, if possible, in the most highly taxed countries, such as Australia and Germany. This strategy reduces the U.S. definition of foreign-source taxable income, since only interest on U.S.-affiliated company borrowings is allocated in proportion to U.S. and foreign assets. Moreover, it attacks the excess foreign tax credit problem directly by reducing foreign taxes paid.

This strategy has received greater attention since the IRS proposed that a U.S. corporation that lends money to a foreign subsidiary must offset its interest expense against any interest income received by such subsidiary before allocating the interest. Direct foreign lending will avoid this further reduction in foreign-source taxable income in the foreign tax credit limitation formula.

Subpart F

The earnings of a foreign corporation not engaged in a U.S. trade or business are not subject to U.S. tax until distributed to U.S. shareholders. Subpart F, however, states that if more than 50% of the shareholders are American, each U.S. shareholder owning 10% or more of the Controlled Foreign Corporation (CFC) must include its share of Subpart F income in its gross income. These amounts are subject to current taxation at the U.S. shareholder level. In general, Subpart F income includes passive income of the CFC as well as income from certain activities likely to be shifted off-shore in order to avoid current U.S. taxation.

The captive insurance industry was a strong target of the Subpart F legislation, which states that when a foreign captive is 25% or more owned by U.S. persons, any U.S. person is liable for current tax regardless of his percentage ownership. Nevertheless, it is still possible to exclude income from current taxation as a result of a de minimis ownership exception that applies when less than 20% of the vote and value is owned directly or indirectly by the primary insured. Furthermore, a de minimis income exception applies when less than 20% of the total insurance income is derived from retired parties.

In general, no income is treated as Subpart F income if a gross foreign base company income is the lower of $1 million or 5% of gross income.

It is clear that opportunites do exist for the U.S. corporation to combat the 1986 Tax Reform Act and to reduce its worldwide tax exposure, by effectively optioning foreign tax credit positions or reinvesting income abroad before repatriation.

17

Prospects for the Future; Prospects for Reform

PROSPECTS FOR THE FUTURE

"The demise of the treaty with the Netherlands Antilles brought a large family of tax-haven possibilities to an end. The slow spread of anti-treaty-shopping clauses in the treaty network of the United States has also narrowed the range of alternatives. Neither tax aversion nor ingenuity have disappeared, however. The quest for tax havens survives, even in the less hospitable present environment. Of the remaining opportunities, the most conspicuous are built around the income tax treaty between the United States and the Netherlands." (Jeffrey Isenbergh, International Tax Planning, 1988.)

The Netherlands tax locating network remains the best and most advantageous for U.S. companies operating worldwide. Interest, royalties and capital gains suffer minimal withdrawal taxes on repatriation to the United States and earnings/dividends also qualify for a participation exemption. The Netherlands is itself a fairly high-tax country, and it might seem at first that successful escape from U.S. taxation under the Netherlands treaty would be little more than trading one problem for another. There are, however, some techniques to reduce Netherlands taxation, arising largely through a surviving income tax treaty between the Netherlands itself and its former colony, the Netherlands Antilles. A combination of entities organized in the Netherlands and the Netherlands Antilles is one of the most promising usable "sandwich" for treaty-favored investment in the United States.

A Dutch "Sandwich"

"Since the repeal of the Netherlands Antilles treaty with the United States, interest paid by a U.S. corporation to a Netherlands Antilles corporation would be subject to U.S. flat-rate withholding tax. If the Netherlands Antilles corporation was incorporated in the Netherlands, however, the interest paid to it by the U.S. corporation would still enjoy treaty exemption. Taxable income in the Netherlands could be offset by deductions for interest paid by a Netherlands corporation. Netherlands withholding taxes on interest paid by the Netherlands corporation could be eliminated if the interest is paid to a resident of a country with which the Netherlands has an income tax treaty." (J. Isenbergh, 1988.)

At this point, the Netherlands Antilles can be employed again. A Netherlands Antilles corporation can be retained in the chain as a holder of debt claims against the Netherlands corporation, in an amount roughly approximating the amount of debt held by the Netherlands corporation in the U.S. corporation.

Exceptions from U.S. controlled foreign corporation status do exist and these exceptions are of prime importance in the deferral and avoidance of U.S. tax on corporations.

A controlled foreign corporation (CFC) is defined in section 957 (a) as "any foreign corporation if more than 50 percent of (1) the total voting power of all classes of stock . . . entitled to vote, or (2) the total value of the stock, is owned . . . by United States shareholders on any day during the taxable year of such foreign corporation." Because more than 50 percent ownership or control is required, an exactly equal partnership between foreign persons and Americans escapes Subpart F.

Specially excluded from Subpart F (see Chapter 16) is income derived by a CFC from shipping in foreign commerce between two points within the foreign country in which CFC is organized and the aircraft or vessels involved are registered. Such operations, even when lightly taxed are not viewed as tax haven transactions but as a commercial activity that happens to be conducted in a low-tax jurisdiction. In contrast, shipping outside national boundaries is treated as a deliberate shift of income to a benign tax regime.

The collapsing corporation (e.g., company formed by foreign investors to make a motion picture in the United States and then before the release of the film to be sold or liquidated) survives, however, because there is a pathway through the Netherlands that leaves open some possibility of a successful collapse. Assume that the ultimate investor first creates and invests capital in a Netherlands corporation ("XYZ"). XYZ would then produce a motion picture in the United States. Production of the motion picture would constitute a U.S. "trade or business" and would also almost certainly involve the creation of a permanent establishment in the United States in the form of a fixed place of business, for example. Rentals derived by XYZ from the subsequent distribution of the motion picture in the United States would run a serious chance of being "effectively connected" with a U.S. trade or business under the Internal Revenue Code. "The Netherlands treaty, however, could shield the rentals from the U.S. corporate tax if XYZ had clearly ended its U.S. permanent establishment before U.S. distribution of the film began and the distribution was carried out through an independent distributor acting in the normal course of business." (J. Isenbergh, 1988.) Although the distribution income would be exposed to the U.S. branch profits tax, despite the ostensible exemption under the Netherlands treaty of business profits not attributable to a permanent establishment, the tax can be avoided with careful planning.

"In Notice 86–17, the U.S. Treasury ruled that the branch profits tax does not extend to the earnings of a foreign corporation in the year in which the corporation completely terminates a U.S. branch business. Under the Notice, the branch can be ended either through the liquidation of the corporation or the sale or repatriation of the branch business assets. In these circumstances, a foreign corporation is not considered to have effectively connected earnings and profits or a decrease in U.S. net equity for the taxable year of termination, and is therefore not subject to the branch profits tax in that year. Thus, if XYZ sells the motion picture and winds itself up and liquidates in the first and only year of the film's distribution, the branch profits tax will be avoided. What this means in the context of the entire transaction is that if XYZ is careful in timing the production, distribution, and sale of a motion picture in the United States, a successful tax-free collapse is still a possibility." (J. Isenbergh, 1988.)

PROSPECTS FOR REFORM

There are six key ways in which the U.S. tax code harms American multinationals doing business abroad. First, it discourages U.S. companies from buying overseas firms, which is the quickest and most obvious way to gain a market foothold. Here the U.S. is at a significant disadvantage when it comes to goodwill, the amount paid in excess of a company's book value in a takeover. Goodwill is not tax-deductible in the United States or the United Kingdom, but it is everywhere else in Europe. Therefore, European companies can easily outbid U.S. companies in acquisitions, knowing that they will receive tax breaks later. To crack the European market, U.S. multinationals must start up their own operations.

A second hindrance is foreign tax credits. Before tax reform, American companies with overseas subsidiaries could consolidate their foreign income into a single basket and get one big credit for most of the taxes they paid to other governments. Now the IRS requires elaborate breakdowns into far smaller baskets by sources of income. Some companies have over 1,000 baskets. Effectively, this makes it harder to use foreign tax credits from one basket to offset the foreign tax bills accumulated in another basket. More baskets mean fewer places to protect foreign income and higher effective U.S. tax rates.

A third hindrance is the treatment of tax incentives, a process known as "tax-sparing." If a U.S. manufacturer sets up a subsidiary in a developing country and is given a tax break from the host government for creating employment opportunities at the new facility, the

U.S. parent will receive no tax credits because the subsidiary pays no foreign taxes. If a German or Japanese company did the same thing, it would receive a tax credit based on the hypothetical foreign taxes the subsidiary would have paid.

A fourth hindrance is the American tax treatment of intercompany transfer pricing, or what a U.S. parent "charges" an off-shore subsidiary for what it makes for the subsidiary. Assume that it costs a U.S. parent $100 to make a widget. It sells the widget to its German subsidiary for $150, and the subsidiary sells it for the equivalent of $200. The parent shows revenues of $150 and profit of $50. At a 50% rate, it pays $25 in American taxes. In Germany, the subsidiary shows revenues of $200 and profit of $50. At a 50% rate, it pays $25 in German taxes. However, the IRS declares that the transfer price to the subsidiary should have been $160 because that is the prevailing U.S. wholesale price, which means a profit of $60 and additional taxes of $30. More recent IRS rules will calculate intercompany transfer prices more aggressively, but many other governments have hinted that they will not accept them. As a result U.S. companies will likely face double taxation. This must be contrasted with a proposed EC rule, effective in 1992, which would automatically take all transfer pricing disputes within the community to binding arbitration.

A fifth hindrance is found in Europe's use of the value added tax (VAT) and its effect on exports. In Europe, a VAT is added at every level of manufacture and distribution and is included in the product's price, very much the way state sales taxes operate in the United States. The VAT is rebated if the product is exported. For example, if an American buys a British suit, the amount of the VAT would be rebated to him. Under U.S. law, there is no VAT on incoming goods. But when a U.S. company exports to Germany, it must pay a VAT in addition to a customs duty. The net effect is that exports by Europeans are made cheaper and exports by Americans are made more expensive. Soon the EC will harmonize its VATs to reduce competition among its member nations and increase restrictions on foreign goods. The U.S. trade deficit will worsen because U.S. companies will be forced to locate their units of production in Europe to obtain the tax benefits of being within the Community.

Finally, the tax treatment of capital gains and dividends is more favorable in Europe than it is under U.S. law. Where U.S. shareholders are taxed on dividends, Europeans receive full or partial exemptions. And while Americans are taxed on their capital gains at a rate similar to ordinary income, many European nations either reduce the rate or exempt capital gains altogether. This will mean proportionally larger pools of money available for financing in the European money markets.

It is clear that in order to stimulate U.S. exports and thus solve the trade deficit nightmare, U.S. legislators need to consider the role off-shore financial centers can play in bringing about a leveling of the international tax playing fields. Unfortunately, U.S. tax legislation discourages U.S. individuals and corporations from attempting to set up operations abroad. Most of the time excess tax is paid abroad, without being fully credited by the IRS, or in the case when new overseas business' losses are separated into different bundles thereby not effectively reducing foreign taxable income to the extent possible. Interest expense allocations further inhibit U.S. corporations from competing effectively with foreign corporations abroad, by being consistently hampered by what the other corporations in the group are borrowing and purchasing.

18

Conclusion

Tax havens have acted as a catalyst for world trade. At present at least 50 per cent of all the world's money is to be found in tax havens or is transferred through them.

It is clear that, if there were no tax haven countries, many products of many multinational corporations would be selling for higher prices, and indeed many of those corporations would not be financially viable. In all likelihood, the consumer would have to bear the tax bills of most transnational and multinational corporations by paying more for their products.

The world of tax havens and off-shore financial centers is an ever-changing one. In all likelihood, the "hot" havens of 1991 will be "overthrown" by a force of many new havens offering better incentives and allowances.

Since the topic of tax havens is so vast and can be said to represent much of the world's trade and financial development, I have endeavored to illustrate the most important and most popular techniques and benefits of using tax havens. As has been shown, users of tax havens cover an enormous spectrum—from the emigrant to the largest corporations in the world, from sports stars to shipping companies.

While the undeniable growth of tax havens is often spoken about, understandably most figures are hard to come by. Some of the figures in the appendices may be slightly out of date, but they should present the reader with an idea as to the site and popularity of many of the world's tax havens.

The fascinating world of tax havens and their uses will continue to play an important role in the business world, while the benefits they provide for individuals' tax planning, particularly individuals (or families) who do not remain in their native land, will undoubtedly increase.

The purpose of global tax planning is not just to reduce tax world-wide but actually to increase a corporation's worth, through cash flow, higher earnings per share, or both. Therefore, the goals of global tax planning must fit into harmony with a company's overall strategic plan. In order to establish a global tax plan, one must under-stand the company and its overall objectives, including such major issues as proposed expansion, any planned new location of facilities, and the development of new products.

As the global economic market changes, new opportunities arise within different countries. Nations develop tax incentive or deferral plans to attract new business. They may even become tax havens, charging little or no income tax. An ongoing objective of a global tax plan is to be alert to the opportunities that exist by creating new entities within such tax-haven jurisdictions. These might include Irish manufacturing companies, Belgian coordination centers, Hong Kong off-shore companies, or Luxembourg holding companies. Therefore, as with any part of the overall strategic plan, global tax planning must be consistently monitored and then updated when necessary.

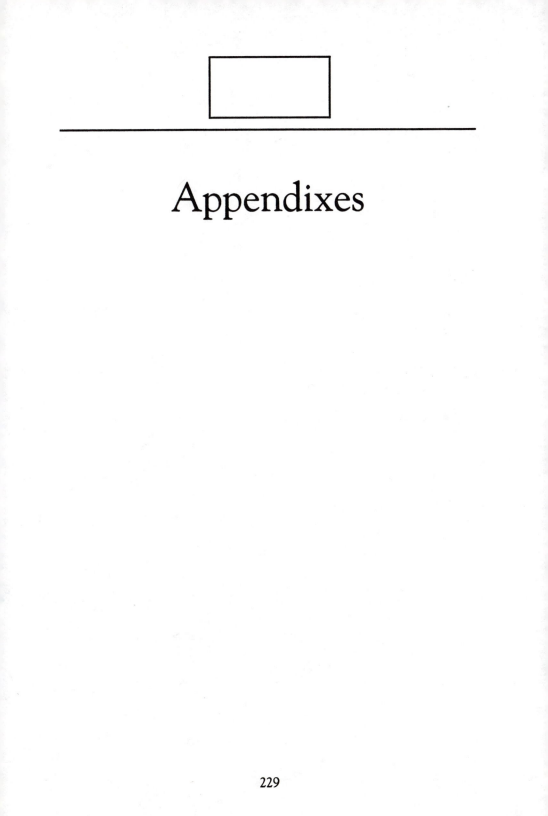

Appendixes

1

A Structure for Australia

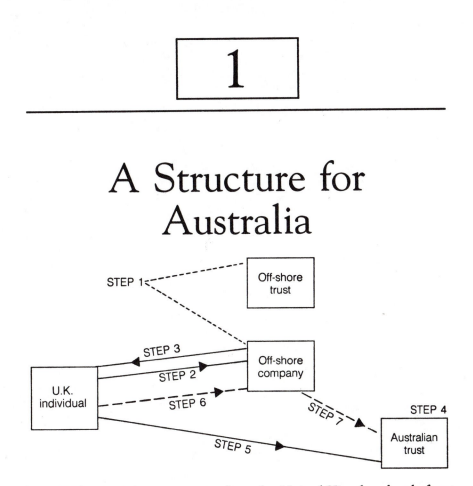

STEP 1 After emigrating from the United Kingdom but before entering Australia, emigrant creates off-shore trust and company.

STEP 2 Blocked assets and income (for life) sold for capital sum to off-shore company on loan account.

STEP 3 Off-shore company that has no cash with which to pay the purchase price, gives promissory note to emigrant.

STEP 4 Prior to taking up residence in Australia, emigrant creates Australian trust of which he is beneficiary.

STEP 5 Emigrant settles promissory note in Australian trust.

STEP 6 Income from blocked funds paid to off-shore company.

STEP 7 Income is paid by off-shore company to Australian trust as repayment of loan and thus not taxable in beneficiary's hands.

2

Publicized Off-Shore Funds Registered and Based in the U.K. Centers: 1972, 1976, 1981, and 1990

Off-shore center	1972		1976		1981		1990	
	No funds	% BI	No funds	% BI	No funds	% BI	No funds	% BI
Jersey	24	60.0	52	55.3	109	51.4	170	47.0
Guernsey	13	32.5	19	20.2	63	29.7	139	38.4
Isle of Man	7	17.5	23	24.5	40	18.9	53	14.6
U.K. Centers	44	51.0	94	60.6	212	69.3	362	

NOTE:
Isle of Man: Total value of funds domiciled £431.6 million.

3

Off-Shore Funds Available in Jersey by Type and Center: 1990

Type of fund	Jersey
Gifts	13
Money market	17
Bonds	20
Commodity	3
United States	12
Far East	22
European	9
U.K. equities	10
International	36
Multiclass	24
Feeder	3
Australian	1
Totals	170

NOTES:
Value of *Public* Jersey domiciled funds under management £7.8 billion.
Total value of all Jersey funds in excess of £10 billion.

Annual U.K. Deposit Levels and Average Deposits per Financial Institution: 1973–90

Year	Jersey			Guernsey			Isle of Man		
	Deposits (£m)	No Inst	Av per inst	Deposits (£m)	No Inst	Av per inst	Deposits (£m)	No Inst	Av per inst
1973	950	34	27,9	279	42	6,6	39	18	2,2
1974	1 060	35	30,3	410	44	9,3	50	19	2,6
1975	1 090	35	31,1	552	45	12,2	119	22	5,4
1976	1 150	39	29,5	631	43	14,7	230	24	9,8
1977	2 250	40	56,3	728	43	16,9	280	27	10,4
1978	3 500	42	83,3	842	42	20,0	315	30	10,5
1979	6 300	45	140,0	1 070	43	24,9	409	32	12,7
1980	7 700	46	167,4	1 800	43	41,9	650	37	17,6
1981	10 000	49	204,1	2 691	42	64,1	837	41	20,4
1982	14 000	42	333,3	3 307	41	80,7			
1983	18 500	43	430,2	4 243	41	103,5			
1984	22 000	45	488,9	5 838	45	129,7			
1985	24 000	45	533,3	7 209	47	153,4			
1986	25 000	52	480,8	9 508	52	182,9	3 194		
1987	26 000	58	448,3	8 838	54	163,7	3 666		
1988	31 000	59	525,4	10 168	56	181,6	4 629		
1989	33 500	59	567,8	12 992	57	227,9	5 841	58	100,7
1990	40 000	63	634,9	15 476	68	198,1			

Source: Jersey Economics Adviser's Office, Guernsey Financial Service Commission: Isle of Man Government

5

New Company Registrations in Jersey: 1978–90

Type of company registered	1978 Number	1978 %	1979 Number	1979 %	1980 Number	1980 %	1981 Number	1981 %	1985 Number	1985 %	1990 Number	1990 %
Trustee, finance and mutual fund companies	51	2,9	46	2,3	35	1,5	38	1,5	56	2,9	107	3,6
Private investment companies	654	37,1	656	32,5	801	35,0	734	29,7	1 101	57,6	1 470	49,3
Jersey residents	102	5,8	88	4,4	71	3,1	58	2,3	89	4,7	60	2,0
British Isle residents	168	9,5	202	10,0	209	9,3	149	6,0	189	9,9	392	13,1
Others	384	21,8	366	18,1	521	22,8	527	21,3	823	43,0	1 022	34,2
Trading companies	1 060	60,1	1 318	65,2	1 452	63,5	1 702	68,9	755	39,4	1 408	47,1
Jersey residents	301	17,1	310	15,3	283	12,4	302	12,2	322	16,8	342	11,4
British Isle residents	256	14,5	310	15,3	300	13,1	322	13,0	302	15,8	229	7,7
Others	503	28,5	698	34,6	869	38,9	1 078	43,6	131	6,9	837	28
Total new registrations	1 765		2 020		2 288		2 474		1 912		2 989	
Total no companies at end year	12 513		13 815		15 210		16 643		21 874		28 131	
No corporation tax companies	3 600		4 215		4 760		5 670					

SOURCE: Commercial Relations Office, Jersey

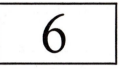

Summary of Taxes in the Main Tax Havens: Tax-Favored Companies

	Withholding tax		Incorporation tax or duty on authorised capital	Annual tax or registration fee	Double tax treaties
	Dividends	Interest			
Netherlands Antilles	None	None	NAG250-2 000	NAG250-2 000	Netherlands, Norway, Suriname, UK, USA
Bahamas	None	None	0,3%	B$1 000	None
Bermuda	None	None	0,25%	Bda$1 000-2 000	USA (limited treaty)
Cayman Islands	None	None	0,5% (CI$850 minimum)	CI$475 minimum	None
Channel Island	20%(1)	20%(1)	0,5% plus £100	£500	Jersey with Guernsey, UK and France, Guernsey with Jersey and UK
Hong Kong	None	None	0,6% (HK$600 minimum)	0,6% (HK$600 min)	None
Liechtenstein	4%(5)	4%(5)(6)	SwF500 plus SwF150 on the second and each additional SwF100 000; plus 2-3% on paid-up capital	0,1% of net worth (SwF1 000 minimum)	Austria(5)
Luxembourg	15%(5) (2.5-10%)(6)	None(8)	1% plus LF4 800	0,2% of issued capital	Austria, Belgium, Brazil, Denmark, Finland, France, Germany, Ireland, Italy, Korea (South), Morocco, Netherlands, Norway, Sweden, UK, USA (all subject to)(5)
Isle of Man	20%	20% (none on bank interest)	0.75%	£500	UK
Panama	10%(5)	None	0,075-0,1% (B20 min)	0,5% (B10 000 maximum plus B150)	None
Switzerland	35% (Nil-20%)(9)	35% (Nil-35%)(9)	3%	Differs according to cantonal laws	Australia, Austria, Belgium, Canada, Denmark, Finland, France, West Germany(7), Greece, Hungary, Ireland, Italy, Japan, Korea (South), Malaysia, Netherlands, New Zealand, Norway, Pakistan, Portugal, Singapore, South Africa, Spain, Sri Lanka, Sweden, Trinidad & Tobago, UK, USA
Vanuatu	None	None	0,078% (Vt40 000 min)	0,078% (Vt40 000 min)	None
British Virgin Islands	15%(1)	15%(1)	$300-1 000	$300-1 000	Denmark, Japan, Norway, Sweden, Switzerland

NOTES:
1 No tax is withheld from payments to non-residents.
2 Except in relation to local real property deals.
3 Local source income or assets only.
4 Non-employed resident aliens.
5 Not applicable to holding or domiciliary companies.
6 Except short-term deposits or loans.
7 Holding companies with large non-Swiss shareholdings may only claim treaty relief in certain circumstances.
8 Except for bond interest which represents a right to profit participation.
9 Treaty rates.

U.K. Company Incorporations and Individual Island Shares: 1978–90*

Isle center	1978		1979		1980		1981	
	No cos	% total	No cos	% total	No cos	% total	No cos	% total
Jersey	12 513	51,6	13 813	49,5	15 210	48,0	16 643	47,5
Guernsey	5 526	22,8	6 162	22,1	6 690	21,1	7 295	20,8
Isle of Man. . . .	6 201	25,6	7 934	28,4	9 772	30,9	11 125	31,7
	24 240		27 909		31 672		35 063	

Isle center	1985		1987		1988		1990	
	No cos	% total	No cos	% total	No cos	% total	No cos	% total
Jersey	21 874	43,9	24 094	40,8	25 131	38,6	28 396	39,4
Guernsey.	9 279	18,6	¹1 106	18,8	12 058	18,5	13 059	18,1
Isle of Man.	18 657	37,4	23 897	40,8	27 843	42,8	30,540	42,4
	49 861		59 097		65 032		71 995	

*End year figures

8

Publicized Off-Shore Funds

	1972	1976	1981	1990
Bermuda	9	15	24	76
Hong Kong	8	20	35	48
Luxembourg	11	11	16	481

9

U.S. Direct Investment Abroad (millions of dollars)

	Direct Investment Position					Capital Outflows (inflows-)					Income				
	1985	1986	1987	1988	1989	1985	1986	1987	1988	1989	1985	1986	1987	1988	1989
European Off-Shore Centers															
Luxembourg	690	802	660	850	904	20	1	-78	392	25	50	105	77	51	116
Netherlands	7,129	11,643	14,842	16,017	17,168	583	3,399	2,051	1,356	906	1,539	2,407	2,974	2,896	2,509
Switzerland	15,766	16,441	19,665	18,357	19,952	578	366	1,787	-1,209	1,682	1,647	1,759	2,797	2,557	3,308
Liechtenstein	350	339	413	377	344	26	-23	73	-11	18	50	50	2	21	10
Western Hemisphere Off-Shore Centers															
Bahamas	3,795	2,991	3,814	4,010	4,463	-62	-828	-250	117	132	974	833	71	305	-99
Bermuda	13,116	15,373	19,215	19,040	17,849	476	1,311	3,331	-580	-1,144	1,293	1,498	1,733	720	2,537
Netherlands Antilles*	-20,499	16,969	14,235	11,633	-6,286	4,235	4,873	3,038	2,959	5,288	-3,077	2,680	-2,083	-1,929	1,508
British West Indies*	3,490	3,794	4,243	3,574	4,404	524	341	184	-698	769	754	609	322	569	477
Asian Off-Shore Centers															
Hong Kong	3,295	3,912	4,389	5,244	5,853	42	720	321	707	370	512	646	1,066	1,139	1,308
Singapore	1,874	2,256	2,384	2,290	2,213	-59	217	226	5	162	383	493	717	853	702
Taiwan	750	869	1,372	1,622	1,949	3	83	367	204	279	92	93	329	348	397

*Cayman Islands predominantly

Source: United States Department of Commerce; Survey of Current Business, August 1990.

10

U.S. Direct Investment Abroad Banking and Finance Sector Combined (millions of dollars)

	1987	1988	1989
European Off-Shore Centers			
Luxembourg	529	289	350
Netherlands	3,006	3,702	3,975
Switzerland	8,014	8,220	8,515
Western Hemisphere Off-Shore Centers			
Bahamas	3,376	3,433	3,459
Bermuda*	18,710	18,384	17,368
Netherlands Antilles*	−14,496	−11,893	−6,600
British West Indies†	4,077	3,396	4,269
Asian Off-Shore Centers			
Hong Kong	2,978	2,006	2,385
Singapore	211	282	153
Taiwan	153	176	278

*Excludes banking sector.
†Cayman Islands predominantly.

Source: United States Department of Commerce; Survey of Current Business, August 1990.

11

Deposit Banks' Foreign
Liabilities and Foreign
Assets and Cross-Border
Bank Deposits
(US$billions)

| | Deposit Banks' | | | | | | Cross-Border Bank Deposits of NonBanks | | | | | |
| | Foreign Liabilities | | | Foreign Assets | | | Residence of Borrowing Bank | | | Residence of Depositor | | |
	1986	1988	1990	1986	1988	1990	1986	1988	1990	1986	1988	1990
European Off-Shore Centers												
Luxembourg	152	200	308	172	232	355	66*	106*	189*	20*	23*	40*
Netherlands	83	110	153	91	121	185	26	35	59	18	34	53
Switzerland	194	243	365	253	319	460	142	173	257	29	35	56
Asian Off-Shore Centers												
Hong Kong	126	270	403	155	310	464	None	None	None	21	24	33
Singapore	171	252	355	162	248	349	35	49	70	3	5	6
Western Hemisphere Off-Shore Centers												
Bahamas	149	165	159	151	163	156	58	56	48	7	8	8
Bermuda	N/A	N/A	N/A	N/A	N/A	N/A	4	5	N/A	11	11	11
Cayman Islands	188	259	330	200	291	342	76	102	133	8	15	27
Netherlands Antilles	5	8	13	6	9	14	3	5	7	14	16	17

*Includes Belgium

Source: IMF: International Monetary Statistics, May 1991

12

Banking in the Bahamas (US$millions)

	1984	1985	1986	1987	1988	1989	1990
Deposit Banks: Assets	32,107	29,423	29,189	39,794	44,487	36,116	33,944
Liabilities	32,135	29,494	29,287	39,909	44,646	36,317	34,151
Branches of U.S. Banks: Assets	94,148	91,390	90,656	104,854	109,722	115,359	103,088
Liabilities	94,979	91,657	92,441	106,805	112,386	117,579	105,864

Source: IMF International Financial Statistics, May 1991

13

Liechtenstein Corporate Taxation an Example

For an AG (company limited by shares) a capital tax of 0.2% is levied. A profits tax is also enforced. The company's net profit is taxable according to the principle of the earnings ratio to taxable capital. The profits tax rate is 50% of the ratio of net profit to taxable capital, but not less than 7.5% and not more than 15% of the net earnings.

Once the tax rate has been determined in this way, it is subject to an increase between 1 to 5% if the payments of the company for dividends, or bonuses exceed 8% of the taxable capital. A maximum surtax of 5% is applied when the payments exceed 24% of the taxable capital. For example

XYZ AG	S Fr
Taxable capital	500,000
Net earnings	120,000
Dividends	105,000

Net earnings represent 24% of the capital, thus a profits tax of 12% will be levied. Since the dividend payment exceeds 20% of the taxable capital, a surtax of 4% is levied. Therefore, the total rate of tax due is 16% of the net earnings: SFr19,200.

Gibraltar Total Bank Deposits (£million)

1987	480.6
1988	743
1989	1,250
1990 (March)	1,350*

*£1,090 million are off-shore deposits, that is, deposits taken from institutions and individuals not resident in Gibraltar.

References

Adams, J. 1983. Coming to terms with the Antilles. *Euromoney*, April.

Avery Jones, JF. 1974. *Tax Havens and Measures against Tax Evasion and Avoidance of the EEC*. London: Associated Business Programmes.

Baig, E. 1984. Whatever became of tax shelters? *Fortune*, 28 May.

Baldwin, T. 1981. Tax Havens and Company Residence. *The Accountant*, 12 February.

Block, S & Sher, G. Tax Partners: Kessel Feinstein. Personal Interviews.

Cain & Co. 1984. *Tax Exemptions for Companies and Trusts in the Isle of Man*. Isle of Man.

    1984. *Isle of Man Guarantee and Hybrid Companies*. Isle of Man.

    1986. *Corporate and Trust Management Services*. Isle of Man.

Campbell, C. 1987. Turtles, Banks and Big Money & A money centre to rival New York and London. Cayman Islands Special Report. *The Times*, 30 October.

Cayman Banks and Trust Companies Law. 1989.

Cayman Islands. 1990, 1986, 1987. Yearbook.

Cayman Islands Government Information Services. 1982. *Advantages of the Financial Centre*.

    1986. *Licensing of off-shore insurance companies*.

    1988. *Economic Development*.

    1988. *Opening a business*.

    1988. *Real Estate & Development*.

    1988. *Registration of Companies*.

Cayman Islands Handbook and Businessman's Guide. The North-wester Co Ltd. 1985-1988. (Annual publication).

Chown, JF. 1974. *Taxation and Multinational Enterprise*. Great Britain: Longman Group.

Chown, JF & Kelen, TF. 1975 *Off-shore Investment Centres*. London: Bankers Research Unit.

Consultrust. Company Site: Switzerland or Liechtenstein?

Deloitte, Haskins & Sells. 1988. *The Channel Islands—A Financial Guide*.

Diamond, WH & Diamond, DB. 1986. *Tax Havens of the World*. New York: Matthew Bender.

Doggart, C. 1985 & 1987. *Tax Havens and their Uses*. London: Economist Intelligence Unit.

Economist. 1983. No Havens from Taxes. *Economist*, 26 March.
    1985. Is off-shore off base? *Economist*, 23 February.

Euromoney. 1987. Bahamas. *Euromoney* supplement, December.
    1989. Treasure Island. *Euromoney* supplement, May.

Financial Mail. 1989. Europe 1992. *Financial Mail*, 12 May (p36).
    1989. 7 July (pp 53-54).

Financial Times. 1987. *Financial Times Tax Newsletter*. Various issues, January.
    1989. July.

Forbes Magazine. 1981. Interested in an off-shore tax haven? *Forbes*, May.

Foreman, T. 1981. Company Residence and Tax Havens. *Accountancy*, March.
    1981. The use and abouse of Channel Islands trusts and companies. *Accountancy*, June.

Grundy, M. 1974. *Grundy's Tax Havens*. 3rd edition. London: Bodley Head/HFL (Publishers) Ltd.

Horwarth & Horwarth International. 1986. *International Tax Planning*. Australia: CCH International.

1987. *Setting up business in Hong Kong.* Australia: CCH International.

1989. *International Tax Planning Marvel.* Australia: CCH International.

Investment International. 1989. The Cayman Islands. *Investment International,* July (pp 35-39).

Jacobs, JD. 1985. *International Tax Summaries.* Coopers & Lybrand. John Wiley & Sons.

Johns, RA. 1983. *Tax Havens and off-shore finance: a study of transnational economic development.* London: St Martin's Press.

Langer, M. 1975. *How to use foreign tax havens.* 5th edition. New York: Practising Law Institute.

Minard, L. 1983. Her Majesty's Tax Haven. *Forbes,* 25 April.

Moore Stephens Organization. Various Internal Publications on the Channel Islands.

Pollard, J. 1986. Tax Havens, CPA *Journal,* April.

Raubenheimer, N. 1989. The Non-Resident Beneficiary. *Wall Street Journal,* July.

Robinson, T. 1983. Next Best Thing to Haven. *Barrons,* 20 June.

Royal Trust. 1985. *Liechtenstein.* 2nd edition. Royal Trust, November.

Spitz, B. 1972. *International Tax Planning.* London: Butterworths.
1988. *Tax Havens Encyclopaedia.* 26th edition. London: Butterworths.

Spring, M & Temkin, J. *International Personal Finance.* Various issues, January 1985-August 1989.

Spurge, J. 1979. *Tax Havens for Corporations.* Houston: Gold Publishing Co.

Tax Management International Foreign Income Portfolios & Tax Management International Journal. 1987 & 1988. Tax Management Inc.

The International. January 1989-August 1989.

Weberman, B. 1981. Haven help us. *Forbes,* 11 May.

1982. Now that's hospitality. *Forbes*, 12 April.

Wener, PS. 1982. A tax haven for migrant traffic. *Businessman's Law.*

1983. Tax Havens and Property. *Businessman's Law.*

Index

265